Ensnared

Know Your Enemy

How to Recognize Satan's Traps
And Overcome Them

By

Monte L. Monk

All scripture quotations are from The Holy Bible: King James Version.

Printed in the United States of America

Ensnared: Know Your Enemy published by

Judah Media Publishing, Mesquite, TX

ISBN-13:978-7372539-0-7

ISBN-10:149534052X

Photography by Judah Media Publishing

Cover design by Judah Media Publishing

Acknowledgments

This book is dedicated to my partners in ministry, love, and life; my lovely wife, Teresa, and my beautiful daughter Tamesha, who supported me with their patience, prayers, and love during the creation of this book. We are forever and, uniquely united. No power in hell or around hell shall be able to separate our family unit. Love you guys 4 ever.

Most importantly, I have to express my sincere gratitude to Mother Versie L. Cleveland, my mother. You told me too never give up on my dreams and you constantly prayed that I would not. Now, this book is the fruit of those prayers. As you can see, family prayer is working. I know when a gauntlet needs to executed on the enemy, I can call you into the fight, and you will not hesitate to engage. Love you always mom.

Dedication

My prayer is that everyone who reads this will find deliverance for their soul, accept Jesus Christ as their Lord and Savior, and live a life of victory through the power of the Holy Ghost.

Table of Contents

Introduction

I watched a YouTube video that showed a hunter carve out a small hole in a rock mound. He then placed some kind of food into the carved out hole. Moments later, a monkey came along, reached into the hole, and grabbed the food. However, the monkey's fist; filled with the food could not be extracted. The monkey began to panic and scream because it could not get free. The hunter, who had hid behind a tree, moved in on the monkey and put a leash around the monkey's neck, and tightened it down. Once the leash was on the monkey's neck, then the monkey let go of the food. The hunter escorted the monkey over to a tree, and began to feed the monkey the food it was trying to eat from the carved out hole.

What was most intriguing about the video was that in the mind of the monkey, it was trapped, even though it was not. It screamed to break free; but it wanted the food; and would not let it go. The monkey magnified its situation by panicking and screaming. Being driven by its desire for the food, it could not see that it really wasn't trapped. But when the hunter actually trapped the monkey, then it let go. Freedom by this time was not an option. The hunter was the only thing that could satisfy its appetites.

Many believers are lured into bondages because of their desire for worldly things, human responses to offenses, spiritual irresponsibility as relates to biblical character or the pressures of life. Every problem and temptation that believers have to deal with on a daily basis is either magnified or minimized by our responses.

Satan will tempt you to respond outside of obedience to the word of God, when temptations and life issues happen. The response that's most appealing to your desire is the one that's presented. If you grab a hold to the wrong thing or act in opposition to the word, deep down in your conscience, you become very aware that the act or response was wrong.

If; for example, you have been offended by someone; you become angry and bitter, and begin to respond in anger; not realizing that the offense has caused you to take hold of bitterness. Like the monkey, you scream and panic, but you won't let go, because you have to respond in kind. You cannot see that the enemy has baited you, and your desire for vindication has distracted you from seeing his plan.

Satan then springs his trap, ties you down with thoughts of resentment and revenge; feeding your mind with his solution of ways that are contrary to the word of God. Now you live your life bitter and angry because of offenses that may have happened months or years ago.

The purpose of this book is to show you how Satan has or will attempt to bait you into sin and bondage by appealing to your desires and emotions. As a follower of Jesus Christ; it's important to recognize that life issues and problems will happen. Satan magnifies these situations and uses them as a means to snare. However, it is imperative to your soul and spirit, if you do not respond according to biblical principles. You will notice throughout this book that many of the demons that are mentioned operate and accommodate each other in their works.

Another point that I will attempt to make is that, your deliverance is determined by your response to your situation. I want you to see that all traps are sprung because of your decision to engage in acts against the word of God. Therefore, it is your obedient response to the word of God, which will make you free.

Remember the monkey was not trapped before the hunter got him. It was only in his mind. He allowed himself to be trapped, pursuing his desire by not letting go. The hunter gave him what he wanted and baited him. You have to know what Satan is using against you to keep you bound. I want you to know your enemy.

My prayer is that as you read this book, your mind will open up and your spirit will be enlightened. You will recognize where you are and call out to God or on behalf of friend who is bound, and that God through Jesus Christ and the power of The Holy Ghost, break the chains and free you or them from the trap and live a life in total victory.

Section I

Understanding Spiritual Warfare

Chapter One

What Is Spiritual Warfare?

What Is Spiritual Warfare

War itself is an organized offensive or defensive effort to defeat or destroy other government entities that pose a threat to a nation's national security. In terms of "spiritual warfare," the fall of Satan and his demons have caused a cosmic war that threatens the souls of humanity and the national security of the kingdom of God on earth. This war is God against Satan, Jesus against the Anti-Christ spirit of Satan, the Christian church against the world system, the children of God against the children of Satan and the Holy Spirit of God against the lust of the flesh.

Warfare describes the military strategies used to undermine the opposition by hindering or stopping the enemy from advancing, by limiting their power, overcoming their forces and finally defeating and/or destroying them. The methods of warfare strategically attack every function of the opposing forces power.

It is important for you to understand the dynamics of spiritual warfare, so you can recognize how the enemy is moving against you, your family, or someone you know. Such strategies involved are:

- Psychological Warfare destroys Christian morale. Satan uses this method against believers by twisting facts into half-truths, lies, spreading rumors and causing arguments, which affects the attitudes and actions of people in your surrounding environment to respond or act towards you negatively. The next phase of this attack affects the Christian mind;

bombarding it with thoughts of anger, depression and/or doubt, brainwashing them into changing their belief system and personality. Ultimately, the Christian loses his will to fight or resist, becoming faint of heart.

- Biological Warfare attacks the Christians' health with physical infirmities *(weakness),* sickness, and disease. This strategy involves a constant repeat of attacks of symptoms that will not go away. The result is incapacity. The Christian loses his mental, spiritual, and physical ability to manage his life and the things of God.

- Information Warfare corrupts the policies of the Christian faith, which is the Word of God. It involves the use of false prophets, teachers, ministers and such the like, in spreading a false and compromising gospel. The Christian is deceived into believing a false gospel that justifies sin, removes accountability and sacrifice; making him weak, mediocre, and non-effective in his spiritual walk.

- Economic Warfare involves attacking the Christians' prosperity. Satan uses this method to attack the Christians resources for living and doing the work of God. The believer's finances are strained through job loss, or lower wages, which affects his/her ability to provide aid for the household. The Christian looks to other means to provide which will draw his mind away from seeking the kingdom of God first.

- Guerilla Warfare involves constant repeated small and large attacks of sabotage, raids, and ambushes of fiery persecutions over a time. Satan uses this strategy to attack you on the job, in your home, in your church, using family members, friends, or familiars. He uses your terrain; the areas in which you dwell and feel safe, to mount attacks that the Christian would never see coming nor expect. This strategy shocks the Christian, immobilizing him in his efforts to live for God.

Through Jesus' birth, life, death, resurrection, and the acceptance of him as your personal Lord and savior, you have overcome Satan and the world. He cannot afford for you to know this, believe it, and keep believing it. Doing so makes you an even greater threat to his kingdom. Therefore, Satan uses these military tactics against you in order to remove the opportunities for victory that you have gained through the blood sacrifice of Jesus Christ.

How Did It Start

> Moreover the word of the Lord came unto me, saying. Son of man, take up a lamentation upon the king of Tyrus, and say unto him, Thus saith the Lord God; Thou sealest up the sum, full of wisdom, and perfect in beauty. Thou hast been in Eden the garden of God; every precious stone was thy covering, the sardius, topaz, and the diamond, the beryl, the onyx, and the jasper, the sapphire, the emerald, and the carbuncle, and gold: the workmanship of thy tabrets and of thy pipes was prepared in thee in the day that thou wast created. Thou art the anointed cherub that covereth; and I have set thee so: thou wast upon the holy mountain of God; thou hast walked up and down in the midst of the stones of fire. Thou wast perfect in thy ways from the day that thou wast created, till iniquity was found in thee. By the multitude of thy merchandise they have filled the midst of thee with violence, and thou hast sinned: therefore I will cast thee as profane out of the mountain of God: and I will destroy thee, O covering cherub, from the midst of the stones of fire. Thine heart was lifted up because of thy beauty; thou hast corrupted thy wisdom by reason of thy brightness: I will cast thee to the ground, I will lay thee before kings, that they may behold thee. Thou hast defiled thy sanctuaries by the multitude of thine iniquities, by the iniquity of thy traffick; therefore will I bring forth a fire from the midst of thee, it shall devour thee, and I will bring thee to ashes upon the earth in the sight of all-them that behold thee. All they that know thee among the people shall be astonished at thee: thou shalt be a terror, and never shalt thou be any more. - Ezekiel 28: 11-19

Lucifer Was Anointed

Before Lucifer's fall, he was the "son of the morning." His name is from the Hebrew word "Heylel" meaning "morning star." The scripture describes him as the "anointed cherub that covered"; giving reference to the two angels that covered the mercy seat, on top of the Ark of the Covenant.

Now to "anoint" means to set someone apart and equip him or her for a special spiritual task of importance. Lucifer, like Aaron and his sons; were anointed and clothed with the holy garments in order to operate in the priest's office before the Lord. Lucifer's anointing was an indication that God personally chose, consecrated, and appointed him to the position of covering or protecting the throne of God.

His Covering

His covering was very interesting. It consisted of precious stones called the sardius, topaz, the diamond, the beryl, the onyx, and the jasper, the sapphire, the emerald, and the carbuncle, and gold: Similarly, this was also the description of the breastplates of judgment worn by the Israelite High Priest, who were also consecrated to work in the temple before the mercy seat.

> And thou shalt make the breastplate of judgment with cunning work; after the work of the ephod thou shalt make it; of gold, of blue, and of purple, and of scarlet, and of fine twined linen, shalt thou make it. Foursquare it shall be being doubled; a span shall be the length thereof, and a span shall be the breadth thereof. And thou shalt set in it settings of stones, even four rows of stones: the first row shall be a sardius, a topaz, and a carbuncle: this shall be the first row. And the second row shall be an emerald, a sapphire, and a diamond. And the third row a ligure, an agate, and an amethyst. And the fourth row a beryl, and an onyx, and a jasper: they shall be set in gold in their inclosings. And the stones shall be with the names of the children of Israel, twelve, according to their names, like the engravings of a signet; every one with his name shall they be according to the twelve tribes. - Exodus 28:15-21

His Workmanship

The third thing to consider is his workmanship. Workmanship comes from the Hebrew "malakah" meaning "ministry" and is the same as "Malak" meaning messenger, Angel, priest or teacher. The scripture never implies that Lucifer was over a choir in heaven; the scriptures just give us a description of his construction, which included instruments: *the workmanship of thy tabrets and of thy pipes was prepared in thee in the day that thou wast created (Ezekiel 28:13)*. God built musical instruments in Lucifer. The viols were the stringed instruments. His pomp was an impressive display of magnificent flaming colors and festive sound. It could be said that when Lucifer spoke, it would sound as if he was singing divine music at the same time.

He was on the holy mountain of God. This was the place where the angels gathered for worship. Walking up and down in the midst of the stones of fire indicated that he stood before the presence of God and His power. He was more than just a musician, he was above all other angels, and was the sum total of perfection. He was designed for worship and ministry on the mountain of God. He was Gods High Priest.

The Fall of Lucifer

The fall of Lucifer was the result of his pride *(Ezekiel 28:12-19)*. Because of his beauty and anointing, he became a narcissist; being caught up in his own image. He assumed that he would be able to exalt himself to the position of being equal with God. Instead, he became a creature of darkness and a terror to humanity.

The multitude of his iniquities, and traffick was indicated by his slander of God. His petty trades of authority and power were offered to the angels, if they should follow and worship him as God. His prideful campaign caused him to transform from Lucifer to "Satan." He became the adversary, the plotter, or the one who devises wicked schemes against everything that is good and called of God. Everything that Lucifer was, he is now the complete opposite. His music is no longer divine, nor glorifies God. He is no longer a High Priest on the mountain of God; he is now a fallen angel desiring to be God, corrupting His word in the church and the world, yet attempting to assume power and a throne while directing worship towards himself through disobedience and rebellion.

This caused a war in heaven, Michael and the archangels battled against him and cast him out. Jesus witnessed this event and testified of his defeat.

> And he said unto them, I beheld Satan as lightning fall from heaven. - St. Luke 10:18

Along with him, fell 1/3 of the heavenly host of angels. Some of these angels are now demons bound in chains in the deep caves of the earth until the day of the final judgment.

For if God spared not the angels that sinned, but cast them down to hell, and delivered them into chains of darkness, to be reserved unto judgment; - 2 Peter 2:4

The Source of Conflict

His fall and lust for power has created conflict. This spiritual conflict is the source of angry disagreements, antagonistic and opposing interests, and ideas in men. The conflict of spiritual warfare has created chaos in the world. It can be seen in natural disasters, wars, family arguments, and brawls.

Everything around us and in us is struggling against evil. This struggle is a constant reminder of the spiritual warfare that is happening around us. Until Jesus returns to end all of Satan's activities, we as the people of God must be aware, and accept the idea that this war is not only spiritual, it also personal and strenuous.

Chapter Two

Personal Warfare

Why is it Personal?

This war is about the spiritual aspects of you, your spirit, and your mind. Your mind is the thing that makes you who you are, what you are, who and what you are in the eyes of God and Satan. The actions you commit are the revelations of your character, which is of course; determined by your mindset. If your mind is corrupt, so will your actions be. Your character and actions determine the condition of your soul. The condition of your soul determines whether you are saved or lost.

Personal conflict started in the Garden of Eden. God issued a command and warning not to eat from the tree of knowledge of good and evil.

> And the Lord God commanded the man, saying, Of every tree of the garden thou mayest freely eat: But of the tree of the knowledge of good and evil, thou shalt not eat of it: for in the day that thou eatest thereof thou shalt surely die. - Genesis 2:16-17

The warning was plain, if he ate from the tree, at that moment; that day, he would surely die *(referring to a spiritual death)*. Man is able to experience life in God through Christ, only by obeying His commands. It is because of this obedience and willing submission to God, that your love for him is proved and manifested.

It is a personal decision to obey or disobey God. Just as well as the command had been the governing principle that mended Adam's and Gods relationship, so shall it be between you and God.

> If ye love me, keep my commandments.-St. John 14:15

Satan's deception of Eve started with a question, "Yea, hath God said, ye shall not eat of every tree of the garden? This question caused Eve to reason or imagine in her mind the thought, "Did God really mean what He said?" the moment she began to entertain this thought, Satan moved in for the kill by removing the consequence of eating from the tree and replaced it with something desirable; something that appealed to the faculties of her flesh. He used a question to bait her interests.

> And the serpent said unto the woman, Ye shall not surely die: For God doth know that in the day ye eat thereof, then your eyes shall be opened, and ye shall be as gods, knowing good and evil. And when the woman saw that the tree was good for food, and that it was pleasant to the eyes, and a tree to be desired to make one wise, she took of the fruit thereof, and did eat, and gave also unto her husband with her; and he did eat. And the eyes of them both were opened, and they knew that they were naked; and they sewed fig leaves together, and made themselves aprons. Genesis 3:4-7

This process snares the soul. You know the commandments, but for the sake of pleasure, you begin to reason within yourself, whether something is wrong or right when compared to the word of God. So then, like Satan, you begin to ask questions like, "where is that or show me that in the word, where God said, "It is a sin?". You start searching for specifics. The root of this dangerous question rests in your flesh and the desire for you to question a known act of sin, so you can justify it. It is a telepathic seed of thought, beamed from the mind of Satan to yours. This is what makes this spiritual conflict personal.

> But I see another law in my members, warring against the law of my mind, and bringing me into captivity to the law of sin which is in my members. Romans 7:23

Apostle Paul had a mind to do the right thing, but the constant pull of his fleshly desires caused him to fall back into sin, fulfilling the lusts of the flesh. Satan will constantly appeal to your desires, tempting you to transgress the word of God. This strategy is the psychological approach in information warfare, designed to twist what you know is right and act against it.

He diminishes righteous thinking by corrupting the word of God that transformed your mind into the mind of Christ. If you give in; your disobedience gives his accusation legitimacy against you, and your testimony of righteousness before God.

Binding the Strong Man

If someone broke into your house and stole your goods, the natural response would be to call the authorities, have the culprits found and arrested, with the hopes of getting your personal belongings back.

> But if I cast out devils by the Spirit of God, then the kingdom of God is come unto you. Or else how can one enter into a strong man's house, and spoil his goods, except he first bind the strong man? and then he will spoil his house. St. Matthew 12:28-29

The gospel is the power of God unto salvation *(Romans 1:16)*. Once you believed the scripture and accepted Christ as your savior, you were snatched from the clutches of sin and Satan. You were the goods, spoiled with the righteousness of God.

> Who hath delivered us from the power of darkness, and hath translated us into the kingdom of his dear Son.-Colossians 1:13

Satan now wants you back, and will do everything in his power to get you; and I mean by any means necessary. He will attack your mind, your emotions and appeal to your innermost desires with the things you once took pleasure in. He will pull every trick in his arsenal and even use the things you trust in, as a means to bait and snare you. You have to remember that you were once his. He still knows what makes you tick.

We all at one time lived in sin and followed the pattern of this world system. Little did we know that we were developing or had developed an intimate relationship with the devil, unknowingly, loving him through obeying his commands by enjoying the pleasures of sin. Now that relationship is severed through your relationship with a newfound love in God, through Christ.

He is like a raging and jealous ex, who will harass you, call you constantly with temptations, even boldly approaching you with gifts of former pleasures from your past life of sinful indulgences. If you do not accept them, he will plot against you, slander you, and even attempt to kill you, if he can. If he cannot have you... no one can. This is personal for him and so should your relationship be with God.

Why is it Strenuous?

This spiritual war for your soul is vigorous and intense. On our part, it requires an aggressive effort to remain prayerful and consecrated. St Luke 18:1 tells us that, "men ought to always pray" in order to keep from fainting, getting discouraged or losing heart in fighting the good fight of faith. Satan never slumbers or takes rests. He is constantly scheming divisive plans to snare your soul. Because of your faith in God through Christ, you will suffer many persecutions.

> Forasmuch then as Christ hath suffered for us in the flesh, arm yourselves likewise with the same mind: for he that hath suffered in the flesh hath ceased from sin; That he no longer should live the rest of his time in the flesh to the lusts of men, but to the will of God. 2 Peter 4:1-2

Most of the trials that you will, and have faced in this life are designed to make you into what Christ has called you to be, but some are designed to trap you, and cause you to lose faith. Suffering persecution comes with the package. Be willing to accept this.

This battle, with or without our consent has drafted us in; leaving us with only two choices; join Satan's army or the army of God. If we choose to follow Christ, then we join Gods army, if we choose not to, you are auto drafted for the opposition. There is no neutral ground. This war is the cause of our trials and tribulations; it is the reason for all wars in the world, society, and our personal lives. Everything is involved in this war and everything is at stake.

Chapter Three

Guerrilla Warfare

Guerrilla Warfare

In chapter one, some of the strategies that Satan uses are summarized. Here, you will you will find a more in-depth look at some of these strategies with scripture references.

This strategy, guerilla warfare, involves attacks from a small group of armed soldiers. The soldiers in these groups could include enemies in an area appearing as friendlies. They do not look like the normal soldier; they are dressed as civilians. However, they are skilled at executing sneak attacks and ambushes. They specialize in sabotage and unexpected raids. They adhere to the element of surprise, destroying and wreaking havoc by quickly and unexpectedly attacking in the open, leaving the enemy in a state of shock. The result of these attacks usually weakens the enemy's strength over time causing them to withdraw.

You can expect persecution from the most unlikely and unexpected sources. These types of attacks, you never see coming because they work through those with whom you know:

- Spouses
- Church brethren
- Friends
- Co-workers

The Familiar or Guerilla Spirit

This strategy is most insidious and spiritually dangerous to the believer, because it works through having soul-ties with the wrong kind of folk. Familiar spirits are imposters, posing as close acquaintances and friends, they may not start out as an enemy, but when God begins to prosper you, because of their weak spiritual condition, or an evil influence in their life, they fall into the trap of jealousy and envy. What Does the Bible Say About This?

> For it was not an enemy that reproached me; then I could have borne it: neither was it he that hated me that did magnify himself against me; then I would have hid myself from him: But it was thou, a man mine equal, my guide, and mine acquaintance. We took sweet counsel together, and walked unto the house of God in company. - Psalm 55:12-14

Jesus experienced this same strategy, which resulted in his crucifixion.

> Mine enemies speak evil of me, When shall he die, and his name perish? And if he come to see me, he speaketh vanity: his heart gathereth iniquity to itself; when he goeth abroad, he telleth it. All that hate me whisper together against me: against me do they devise my hurt. An evil disease, say they, cleaveth fast unto him: and not that he lieth he shall rise up no more. Yea, mine own familiar friend, in whom I trusted, which did eat of my bread, hath lifted up his heel against me. But thou, O LORD, be merciful unto me, and raise me up, that I may requite them. Psalm 41:5-10

The familiar spirit is rooted in witchcraft. They were and are cunning demons that would usually appear in different disguises or forms of animals, and sometimes humans, whenever they aided a witch in devising a potion or spell. The term "familiar spirit" is not mentioned much in the church world today, even though they were and are prevalent in old and New Testament times. Today you know them as false teachers and preachers of the gospel. They are the imposters. In secular terms, they are called "frenemies."

In the Old Testament, God was specific in His commands to the children of Israel not to deal with necromancers, charmers, consulters with familiar spirits, or wizards *(Spiritism)*.

They pretend to be friendly in the workplace, happy for your home life, and preach, and worship like a true worshipper, but they are your rivals. They are the guerrilla soldiers assigned by Satan to enter your terrain, your circles and disturb the glory and favor that God has placed in your life. They are there to disrupt your prosperity and peace in the workplace, destroy your home life, and cause disunity in a fellowship of believers. They are the aids to the master witch manipulator, the devil.

The Soul Tie

The Familiar or impostering spirit works insidiously because of the soul-tie. The soul tie is a spiritual and mental link or cleaving that holds two or more people together that could bring about negative or positive results. The ties are formed through deep conversations and emotional, caring connections; having like-minded ideas and goals. In relationships, they are formed through sexual encounters.

David and Jonathan – Mutual Faith

> And it came to pass, when he had made an end of speaking unto Saul, that the soul of Jonathan was knit with the soul of David, and Jonathan loved him as his own soul. And Saul took him that day, and would let him go no more home to his father's house. Then Jonathan and David made a covenant, because he loved him as his own soul. And Jonathan stripped himself of the robe that was upon him, and gave it to David, and his garments, even to his sword, and to his bow, and to his girdle. - 1 Samuel 18:1-4

Some have said that this relationship signified a homosexual relationship between Jonathan and David. This is far from the truth. These young souls were tied together because of a mutual faith in the things of God. Jonathan admired the strength and courage of David. Jonathan was moved by David's victory over the Philistines and the giant, Goliath without the use of a sword and the confidence he showed in God, through his testimony of faith before the battle (1 Samuel 17:1-58).

David and Saul – A Dangerous Soul Tie

Let's not forget that King Saul was also drawn to the soul of David. Saul admired him so much so, that he would not let David return to his home. Saul made him a captain over his army and took him everywhere he went. However, an evil spirit troubled Saul, because of His former disobedience to the will of God. This spirit stirred a grievous spirit of Jealousy when the women proclaimed more victories for David over Saul.

> And Saul was very wroth, and the saying displeased him; and he said, They have ascribed unto David ten thousands, and to me they have ascribed but thousands: and what can he have more but the kingdom? And Saul eyed David from that day and forward. And it came to pass on the morrow, that the evil spirit from God came upon Saul, and he prophesied in the midst of the house: and David played with his hand, as at other times: and there was a javelin in Saul's hand. And Saul cast the javelin; for he said, I will smite David even to the wall with it. And David avoided out of his presence twice. – 1 Samuel 18:8-11

This is a perfect example of why you should be careful of whom you follow and connect too. Saul was a man of power, authority, and position. However, he was not right with God. After this jealous spirit took over Saul, many others spirits became prevalent. He was moved with anger, wrath, and soon malice. Saul eyed David, looking for an opportunity to attack and kill him. David went on with Saul as he normally did, playing the harp. However, when the opportunity to kill David presented itself, Saul executing his premeditated plan, threw the javelin at David to Kill Him.

In the Workplace

The guerilla is the one who wants your position, will ask you questions concerning a task that they already know the answer too but wants to see if you knew it. They will often do this or show some kind of skill they know you do not have, in front of the boss in order to make you look bad, while raising themselves up. The guerilla or familiar will go out to lunch with you, cry with you, talk with you but will insult you by twisting compliments. When you speak on a topic, they will interrupt with another topic or brush you off as if they are busy. They will offer "friendly criticism' but never give a true compliment. They always seem to be in competition with you. If you have an idea for something, they shoot it down with doubts.

The familiar spirit or guerilla within the frenemy, at some point will release their true nature. They sabotage your plans, secretly report mistakes by shifting or implying the blame on you. You will even find them discussing your faults to other co-workers. You know they do this, because they have discussed other co-workers faults with you. David never paid attention to Saul eyeing him. This was a clear sign that Saul was ready to release his true nature against him. You have to watch who your friends are. Be aware of who's watching you.

The Family

One of the most dangerous types of guerilla or familiar spirits is the one that is living in the house with you. The guerilla or familiar spirit in marriage is the result of insecurity and jealousy of the other spouse. An example would be a woman who has more education; financial stability and a strong foundation to make it on her own, can become a perceived threat to her husband or vice versa.

The threat starts in his mind. The husband may sincerely love his wife, but her qualities stand out more than his do. The guerilla or familiar spirit in the spouse will take advantage of this and manifests itself when the husband ceases to compliment his spouse, but demeans her character and her looks. He makes suggestions about her quitting her job and working at home, becoming more of a homemaker than assisting with the finances. He wants to see her on a lower level than he is. When she wants attention, he brushes her off, but is quick to provide attention to an outside friend. This is dangerous, if it is not handled quickly. Usually, these types of relationships could become violent and end in violence.

Guerillas in the family could be another family member that you trust discussing your home life too. Later, you find out, that your home life issues are discussed among other family members, you are left out of invitations to family events, your children are treated different from others, and you do not get family visitors to your home, except for when you are ready to discuss your business. These types of familiars cause family disputes, which in the end creates bitterness and tears, tearing down the unity within the family unit.

The Church

You go to church and the pastor calls you up to the front of the church, and under the guise of prophesying, he calls out all of your shortcomings, embarrassing you in front of the congregation. He starts this expose, by saying, "the lord said" and ends this tirade of insults by ending it with an appeal for you to get right. Because of the pain and shock over the event, you are blinded to the previous conversation you had with him or her about the very issues discussed. Because of your trust in leadership and your attempt to be a good Christian, you never knew that you were dealing with a person who had a guerilla or familiar spirit.

Then there is the other scenario where you confided in a brother or sister in your fellowship, and discovered that your business has been discussed with others and the news of your discussion with your so-called friend has somehow spread among the congregation. A guerilla or familiar spirit has exposed you.

The Counter Strategy

The Church

Understand and expect that even the most powerful men are to be less trusted. Man is subject to error and emotions that can lead him to making the wrong decisions and act in accordance with the wrong spirit. This even applies to your church leaders. We are only to follow men as they follow Christ. These evil times require us to trust in God and his discernment. Look at what happened in the days of Micah, the prophet.

> Trust ye not in a friend, put ye not confidence in a guide: keep the doors of thy mouth from her that lieth in thy bosom. For the son dishonoureth the father, the daughter riseth up against her mother, the daughter in law against her mother in law; a man's enemies are the men of his own house. Therefore, I will look unto the Lord; I will wait for the God of my salvation: my God

will hear me. Rejoice not against me, O mine enemy: when I fall, I shall arise; when I sit in darkness, the Lord shall be a light unto me. - Micah 7:5-8

The people forsook their beliefs in God and His covenants with them. The character of righteousness faded in the lives of those who claimed to be covenant keepers. This caused a rise in bloodthirsty pursuits of snaring one another into traps. The main culprits were the religious leaders. The word used to describe how they set the traps is "sharpness." Webster's Dictionary defines this as, "having exceptional discernment and judgment, especially in practical matters" and "the state or quality of being able to sense light impressions or differences."

The evil works that were done by the leaders of that day was that they joined to exercise evil on the people. Micah describes their works as briers and thorns, meaning that they entangled the people in strife's and pierced family unity and loyal friendships, using the knowledge of the their situations; and taking advantage of them by causing division. They confused an entire nation, operating under the influence of a familiar spirit.

To counter this strategy you must trust in the Lord. I am not discounting leadership. The bible teaches that we need leaders in order to be perfected and edified:

> And he gave some, apostles; and some, prophets; and some, evangelists; and some, pastors and teachers; For the perfecting of the saints, for the work of the ministry, for the edifying of the body of Christ: Till we all come in the unity of the faith, and of the knowledge of the Son of God, unto a perfect man, unto the measure of the stature of the fulness of Christ: That we henceforth be no more children, tossed to and fro, and carried about with every wind of doctrine, by the sleight of men, and cunning craftiness, whereby they lie in wait to deceive. - Ephesians 4:11-16

When it comes to your leaders and fellow brethren, you must raise your level of discernment. Discernment is the power to recognize and see into the spiritual realm by using the word of God through the Holy Ghost. This is not a mystical process. It is simply using righteous judgment by applying the life of the people in your circles to the word of God.

Leaders are supposed to build up the spiritual man of those that follow him. Even your fellow believers are supposed to do the same. Included in building the spiritual man, sometimes, rebuke is necessary but not embarrassment. If rebuke is the only means of edification, then you may be dealing with a familiar or guerilla spirit.

Also, be wary of those in your fellowship who seem to seek and possess knowledge of many within the congregation. Familiar or Guerilla spirits, at some point will cause confusion. They spread gossip secretly, always having some secret knowledge to share about somebody else. Here is a rule of thumb: If they tell other people's business, why wouldn't they share yours? In most cases, those that have this spirit are up to something evil. Even if it is, just to spread gossip. The gossip that is spread could damage that fellow believer's reputation among other Christians and possibly murder them spiritually. The stories they carry after a while, will lose its consistency, resulting in a half-truth, which is still, a lie and we know that Satan is the father lies.

> And withal they learn to be idle, wandering about from house to house; and not only idle, but tattlers also and busybodies, speaking things which they ought not. - 1 Timothy 5:13.

The Workplace

The operation of this spirit operates just about the same at work; therefore, handling this kind of spirit will require the same strategy that you would use in your fellowship. At work, the guerilla will befriend you first and start conversations with you in order to find out your mindset about certain things. The same rule applies, "you will know them by their fruits." The key is not to be tricked by the outward appearance, the smile, the invitations to lunches, even the support they give you in workplace confusion. The familiar, guerilla spirit is a frenemy. One of the traits that you have to look for is the "backbiting and talebearing tongue."

> Thou shalt not go up and down as a talebearer among thy people: neither shalt thou stand against the blood of thy neighbour; I am the LORD. - Leviticus 19:16

Those who possess this spirit will talk about others in the office, the previous write-ups and terminations or who is about to be terminated. They know all the office gossip. You can rest assured that if they know all this stuff about everybody else and telling you about it; they will surely gain information about you and spread it.

The talebearer is one who carries and tells secrets of others, whereas the backbiter is one who tears down the reputation of another behind their back, using slander. So how do you rid yourself of this kind of company?

> The north wind driveth away rain: so doth an angry countenance a backbiting tongue. - Proverbs 25:23

An angry look and posture will surely send the signal that you are not interested in such talk and information. Most likely, the spirit will take a stronger and bold stand to resist your response.

> Moreover if thy brother shall trespass against thee, go and tell him his fault between thee and him alone: if he shall hear thee, thou hast gained thy brother. But if he will not hear thee, then take with thee one or two more, that in the mouth of two or three witnesses every word may be established. And if he shall neglect to hear them, tell it unto the church: but if he neglect to hear the church, let him be unto thee as an heathen man and a publican.- St. Matthew 18:15-17

The scripture is referring to unruly brethren in your fellowship that has trespassed against you. However, the same process can be used in the workplace against the guerilla. The guerilla spirit will never see it coming; that is your response. Do not be afraid to speak out when you are approached. Let them know upfront, that you are not interested in such talk and information and what they are doing is wrong and will only cause confusion in the workplace. If the person continues to do so, take the issue to management and pray.

In the Family

If you have detected a familiar spirit in your spouse, the answer to the problem rests in your marriage vows. The women can defeat this spirit simply by being a good wife and respecting his position as the husband:

> Likewise, ye wives, be in subjection to your own husbands; that, if any obey not the word, they also may without the word be won by the conversation of the wives; While they behold your chaste conversation coupled with fear. Whose adorning let it not be that outward adorning of plaiting the hair, and of wearing of gold, or of putting on of apparel; But let it be the hidden man of the heart, in that which is not corruptible, even the ornament of a meek and quiet spirit, which is in the sight of God of great price. For after this manner in the old time the holy women also, who trusted in God, adorned themselves, being in subjection unto their own husbands: Even as Sara obeyed Abraham, calling him lord: whose daughters ye are, as long as ye do well, and are not afraid with any amazement.- 1 Peter 3:1-6.

Do not strive in arguments, but submit yourself to prayer and God and remember his status as the husband; he is the head of the family, he is the leader. To rid your home and husband of this spirit, it will require your loving commitment to him, and a constant reminder of how much you appreciate him. Your husband is blinded to who you are because of the evil spirit. It is up to you to remind him of who you are and how you feel.

Husbands, the same rule applies. It is through your love for her that you can win her over from this spirit and keep your home in Godly order. Do not mistake the phrase, "giving honour unto the wife, as unto the weaker vessel" as a reference to her being inferior. This is far from the truth. The wife was not designed as an inferior being. She was designed to be a "help suitable" for your support, standing by your side and assisting you in times of trouble.

You have to show her the utmost respect and love; proving to her that everything you do is for her and the home. Your success is her success. You have to dwell with her according to knowledge; that is the knowledge of the word and what you know of her. You know her true character and love for you. Cater to that. After all, at the end of the day, she is a reflection of your strength.

In the case of outside family members, what you want to avoid is offense and bitterness. You accomplish this by seeking peace with the offending member. Let them know that you have noticed how you and your family is treated and would like to know why and solve the issue. If peace does not abide, the next best solution is not to share your information with the family member and avoid confrontations. God has called us to peace.

Chapter Four

Psychological Warfare

This strategy is designed to hamper and defeat the enemy's ability to make decisions. It is an attack on the enemy's think tank, which paralyzes the moral and physical capacities of the unit, causing them to be uncoordinated, ineffective, and discouraged.

This strategy deals in propaganda, which is a conglomerate of deceptive tactics involving lies, assumptions, and accusations. The usage of the information is to vilify or embarrass the enemy by negatively influencing and manipulating the audience's views of the opposing force and directing the audience's beliefs in favor of the accuser. The result of such strategy is that the opposing force is bombarded with severe ridicule and hatred from the audience. They are then forced, by public opinion and outrage, to change its methods, beliefs and reason for opposition; succumbing to the rules and requests of the accuser.

Evil Surmisings

In psychological warfare, the accusations are made up of "evil surmising's". Webster defines "surmising" as supposing something is true without having the necessary evidence to confirm it. These are scandalous conclusions based on suspicious thoughts, ideas, and events that lack the necessary evidence that would deem an accusation true. Therefore, when a person surmises evil against you, they assume that you are guilty of sin without the evidence. There evidence against you is only superficial. It is based on what is considered obvious but not complete. An example of such an act can be found in Amos 7:10-13:

> Then Amaziah the priest of Bethel sent to Jeroboam king of Israel, saying, Amos hath conspired against thee in the midst of the house of Israel: the land is not able to bear all his words. For thus Amos saith, Jeroboam shall die by the sword, and Israel shall surely be led away captive out of their own land. Also Amaziah said unto Amos, O thou seer, go, flee thee away into the land of Judah, and there eat bread, and prophesy there: But prophesy not again any more at Bethel: for it is the king's chapel, and it is the king's court.

Amos preached against the religious and political system of that day and offended Amaziah, the priest who conducted calf worship in the sanctuary at Bethel. He "surmised" an evil accusation to Jeroboam claiming that Amos was committing treason by preaching words against him and disrupting the peace within the land. His accusation was false. It was a half-truth. According to verse nine, Amos said, "God would come against the house of Jeroboam with the sword," this indicated justice. However, Amaziah stated in verse eleven, that Amos said, "Jeroboam shall die by the sword, and Israel would be led captive out of their own land." The prophecy of Amos was really directed at the false god worship that was taking place a Bethel. Amaziahs' accusation was a twist of words; deceiving Jeroboam. What was true about his surmise was that the Sanctuary at Bethel did not belong to God; it did belong to the King due to the worship of false gods.

As a believer in Christ, whenever you stand for truth and speak out against evil doing. The enemy will exercise this strategy against you in order to the turn people's ideas and thoughts about you into a negative. The more you stand for Christ on your job, in your home, and even within your fellowship, you will and should expect to suffer being falsely accused and being misunderstood. Accusations will be made against you. Those who have an evil heart will twist your words in a situation and desire to see you removed.

> Beloved, think it not strange concerning the fiery trial which is to try you, as though some strange thing happened unto you: But rejoice, inasmuch as ye are partakers of Christ's sufferings; that,

26

when his glory shall be revealed, ye may be glad also with exceeding joy. If ye be reproached for the name of Christ, happy are ye; for the spirit of glory and of God resteth upon you: on their part he is evil spoken of, but on your part he is glorified. But let none of you suffer as a murderer, or as a thief, or as an evildoer, or as a busybody in other men's matters. Yet if any man suffer as a Christian, let him not be ashamed; but let him glorify God on this behalf. - 1 Peter 4:12-16

The purpose of this strategy is to discourage you, stop your spiritual development, and work for God. On the other hand, it operates to deceive the hearer; leading them, down a path of deception where their perceptions of spiritual things concerning you are distorted by lies. The constant slander and defamation of character caused by evil surmising's can lead you into frustrations, which ultimately leads you into becoming spiritually, mentally and physically fatigued, bringing your spiritual development and work for God to a halt. Like Amaziah, in the church world, people who commit to using this strategy against you has somehow become offended by your testimony and walk with God. In the workplace, it could be the favor of God manifested in your display of skill, which brings prosperity and notoriety from upper management. In your home, it could be the change of atmosphere, because of your prayers and submission to God, which has disrupted the principalities and evil forces, which work against your home through family members, who are not saved or weak in the faith.

The only way the enemy can use such a strategy against you, he has to find a person with an evil heart. According to St. Luke 6:45, Jesus said, "an evil man out of the evil treasure of his heart bringeth forth that which is evil: for out of the abundance of the heart his mouth speaketh. The pawns in psychological warfare seem to always know the latest gossip and act as busybodies carrying and gaining information from one to source to another. The gossip contains slander, the lessening of another person's character. These type of people are insensitive to the trials and sinful pasts of others. They are the evil gatekeepers that make constant attempts to destroy the entryway to unity among believers, in the workplace and in the home. They rarely can hold a conversation about Godly things and if they do, they somehow connect it with some kind of slander about a person you know.

> If any man teach otherwise, and consent not to wholesome words, even the words of our Lord Jesus Christ, and to the doctrine which is according to godliness; He is proud, knowing nothing, but doting about questions and strife's of words, whereof cometh envy, strife, railings, evil surmisings, Perverse disputings of men of corrupt minds, and destitute of the truth, supposing that gain is godliness: from such withdraw thyself. - 1 Timothy 6:3 6

The words of a slanderer, backbiter, or talebearer can bring about many trials in your life. Even though they are orchestrated by the devil, God allows this temptation to rise against you to prove your faith in Him. God already knows whether you will be faithful to him or not, so the trials are for you to be convinced of your identity in Christ, in your mind. Now this does not mean that the devil is not in the details. You may have believed that Satan has to have permission to attack you. You are misinformed my friend. He is the adversary of God. He hates everything that is associated with God. If war were now being fought in the cosmos between God and Satan, why would he seek permission to destroy something that belongs to God?

When it comes to the believer, Satan does not seek or need permission to attack you, he is limited in the attack itself. He cannot overtake your free will; he has to break you down so you would give in to his will. The Parable of the sower reveals this:

> But he that received the seed into stony places, the same is he that heareth the word, and anon with joy receiveth it; Yet hath he not root in himself, but dureth for a while: for when tribulation or persecution ariseth because of the word, by and by he is offended. - St. Matthew 13:20-22

Avoid Bitterness

Experiencing this type of warfare can yield feelings of anger, frustrations, and bitterness. The snare of this strategy is to fill your mind with negative self-talk that say, 'how can they do this me?". Once you begin to focus on your offense, you have been baited into the trap. Satan's plan is to plant in you a root of bitterness. This is what the seed of offense yields, in the heart of the Christian

Usually, your first response would be to leave your church. You will not leave your family, nor your job, that is too significant to you. It is nothing for you to leave and change your church. This does not solve the problem. Offense is a heart problem. The enemy will heighten your feelings of offense towards your church, your brethren and your leaders, your family and those in the workplace because he wants to stop the work of God from going forth through your example of righteousness, ruining the effectiveness of your testimony in the world. The church is your hub, your filling station for power. I am not saying to remain under an abusive ministry, if you decide to leave; purge the offense first through reconciliation. Forgive. If there is no remedy, then leave and find another spirit-filled church.

Counter the Attack

Preparation for this type of attack is to realize that persecution comes with the package of salvation. The problem is not you; it is who and what you believe in that is the source of your problem. Satan wants you to believe that what your suffering is a result of your failings, lack of qualifications, church standards not being met or you are doing something wrong as it relates to God and His will for your life. This is far from the truth. All of this is a spiritual attack on your mind. It is Psychological.

As you seek to line up your life with the principles of faith, you will witness persecution coming from some of the most unexpected sources, such as:

- Family: Husband, wife, children, mother, father,
- Friends: People you grew up with, best friends, schoolmates
- Workplace: Your boss, fellow co-workers, supervisors
- Churches: Brothers, sisters, people you have confided in, leaders and pastors

Think not that I am come to send peace on earth: I came not to send peace, but a sword. For I am come to set a man at variance against his father, and the daughter against her mother, and the daughter in law against her mother in law. And a man's foes shall be they of his own household. St. Matthew 10:34-36

Anytime, anywhere, where there is righteousness, you can expect resistance. That resistance is the cause of suffering.

The "world" or "Thalassa" which includes fallen humankind and this present world system is at odds with the Kingdom of God and the followers of Jesus Christ.

> If the world hate you, ye know that it hated me before it hated you. If ye were of the world, the world would love his own: but because ye are not of the world, but I have chosen you out of the world, therefore the world hateth you. Remember the word that I said unto you, the servant is not greater than his lord. If they have persecuted me, they will also persecute you; if they have kept my saying, they will keep yours also. But all these things will they do unto you for my name's sake, because they know not him that sent me. If I had not come and spoken unto them, they had not had sin: but now they have no cloak for their sin. He that hateth me hateth my Father also.-St. John: 15:18-23

You have to be willing to suffer for the cause of Christ. You must "arm" yourself with this mindset. *(1 Peter 4:1-4)* It is your cross. Once you have accepted this idea, it makes dealing with persecution much easier to be accepted and easier to overcome it. It is for your making.

God uses persecution as a process of humbling the soul before Him, driving the believer to a total dependence upon His spirit and word of deliverance. It is during this process that you receive a greater grace *(divine assistance)* from God to help endure.

Persecution is designed to keep you from yielding to the temptations of the flesh. When these temptations arise, even from the people that you have in your circles; your loved ones, friends and coworkers, it will cause you to recognize the strategies of the enemy at work. Remember the promises of God. In them, you have an assurance of deliverance.

> Many are the afflictions of the righteous: but the Lord delivereth
> him out of them all. - Psalms 34:19

So even when the enemy uses this tactic against you; God is "allowing" it to happen in your favor. It is for your spiritual growth. It is a test of your faithfulness to see whether you will trust God and His word.

The key to winning against this strategy is endurance, by not forgetting the promises of deliverance. Adversities will come in the lives of both sinner and saint. Nevertheless, as a born again believer, you have an advantage; and that is the word of God and the power of His might.

Rise Above Your Affliction

> Likewise, the Spirit also helpeth our infirmities: for we know not
> what we should pray for as we ought: but the Spirit itself maketh
> intercession for us with groanings, which cannot be uttered. And
> he that searcheth the hearts knoweth what is the mind of the
> Spirit, because he maketh intercession for the saints according to
> the will of God. And we know that all things work together for
> good to them that love God, to them who are the called according
> to his purpose. - Romans 8:26-28.

Counter this attack by building your spiritual man through prayer. This is how the spirit of God will help you get a grip on your spiritual and physical discouragements and/or infirmities. These afflictions and persecutions can be so overwhelming on the mind. You can lose focus on what you should pray for. However, the spirit of God will search the heart; that is the deep recesses of your mind and interpret the groans and moans of your afflictions to God. This is what it means by, "but the Spirit itself maketh intercession for us with groanings which cannot be uttered. And he that searcheth the hearts knoweth what is the mind of the Spirit, because he maketh intercession for the saints according to the will of God "Therefore, your counter move would be to pray and sincerely ask God for His help.

Integrity

When you are offended by false accusations, I understand that your first response would be retaliate by using the same tactics and confronting the accuser in a much unpleasant fashion. My recommendation is "no don't do that!" This is what the enemy wants. He wants you to respond in kind. Vengeance is the Lords.

> Dearly beloved, avenge not yourselves, but rather give place unto wrath: for it is written, Vengeance is mine; I will repay, saith the Lord. - Romans 12:19

God wants you to walk with integrity and display excellent and unchallenged Christian character. You have to resist the devil and prove that you are morally principled, strong in the faith, and undivided in your mind. Your actions will prove that the slanderer is being used of the devil. Remember, even though the words hurt, and have painted a dim picture of you, a life read is more impacting and influencing in the audience mind. Maintain your integrity

> The righteousness of the perfect shall direct his way: but the wicked shall fall by his own wickedness. The righteousness of the upright shall deliver them: but transgressors shall be taken in their own naughtiness. - Proverbs 11:5-6

Chapter Five

Economic Warfare

This strategy involves attacking or threatening to attack a country's' economic status for weakening its political and military might. The opposing country causes an adversary to change its policies or behavior through threats of capital asset freezing, aid suspension or the use of sanctions. Goods are restricted and financial opportunities are withheld. The results of such warfare will cause a nation to fall into starvation and homelessness. Sickness and disease spread rapidly, due to limited access to medicines and advances in medical technologies. How does this affect you?

This strategy involves an attack on your prosperity and health. Remember, the focus of Satan's demonic attacks is to rid you of your ability to fight back and take away your testimony in Jesus Christ and your desire to live for God. Coupled with this intention is to hinder or stop your spiritual influence in the world. He has to change your behavior and political policy, which is the word of God.

> Beloved, I wish above all things that thou mayest prosper and be in health, even as thy soul prospereth. - 3 John 1:2

It is Gods will that you prosper and be in health. However, the key to this is that your soul must prosper in God also. Here is a scenario:

You paid your tithes and offerings faithfully. You have never missed and reaped the blessing of doing so. You have a nice vehicle; there is nothing wrong with that. You have a nice home; there is nothing wrong with that, you have a decent amount of credit card debt. You dress in the finest clothes; there is nothing wrong with that. Then you suffer a pay cut or you lose your job.

Now you are facing foreclosure, you struggle to make the payments on your vehicle; your car has been or is under the threat of repossession. Your refrigerator and cupboards look at little bare, and the bills just keep rolling in. Now you believe that this is not supposed to be happening to you, because you pay your tithes and give your offerings.

Now let's look at the situation a little closer. Your mortgage has a high interest rate; your vehicle has a high interest rate and a long-term contract..., let's just say seven years. Your bank account is nearly dry because during the time of your prosperity, you never bothered to save any money or build an emergency fund. You shopped every pay period because you felt you deserved the best. This is what God wanted for you; at least, that is what the preacher said. Time has gone by and now you cannot shop as you used to, your vehicle has been repossessed, and your home is in foreclosure. You have a mountain of debt and unpaid bills. You dread going to church because you are required to pay your tithes, but you have bills, you are tempted to use those monies for other things. Because of a reduction in funds, aid in your home has been cut off or minimized, hindering you from providing for your family. Discouragement has set in and now you are wondering, "What did I do wrong for God to allow this to happen to me?" You paid your tithes and according to the doctrine, you are not supposed to suffer this type of lack.

The worry and stress of things bring about headaches and sickness. You become weak and spiritually frail. You lack the motivation to do something about yourself. Obesity or weight loss becomes an issue in your life. You need health care but cannot afford it, diabetes, heart disease, high blood pressure or such the like begin to threaten your life.

You have a family that needs to be provided for. You know something has to be done. Therefore, you set out looking for work, and new income because, you have to restore everything that you have lost. Opportunities have presented themselves, better than nothing right, but they take you away from church and your work for God. You find yourself missing service more and more until soon, you have stopped going altogether. What happened? You were snared.

> And these are they which are sown among thorns; such as hear the word, And the cares of this world, and the deceitfulness of riches, and the lusts of other things entering in, choke the word, and it becometh unfruitful. - St. Mark 4:18-19

The dangers of this strategy is that it leads you to believe that you have not left God, blinding you to the fact that your faith has become dormant, leaving you to rely on your own abilities to provide.

Your desire to attain the things you have lost is what's driving you and even if you gain it back, through self-help methods, motivational speeches, tapes and books about success, God has been choked out. There is a danger that lies ahead that Satan does not want you to see.

> Every branch in me that beareth not fruit he taketh away: and every branch that beareth fruit, he purgeth it, that it may bring forth more fruit. Now ye are clean through the word, which I have spoken unto you. Abide in me, and I in you. As the branch cannot bear fruit of itself, except it abide in the vine; no more can ye, except ye abide in me. I am the vine, ye are the branches: He that abideth in me, and I in him, the same bringeth forth much fruit: for without me ye can do nothing. If a man abide not in me, he is cast forth as a branch, and is withered; and men gather them, and cast them into the fire, and they are burned. If ye abide in me, and my words abide in you, ye shall ask what ye will, and it shall be done unto you. Herein is my Father glorified, that ye bear much fruit; so shall ye be my disciples - John 15:2-8

Financial Responsibility

The prosperity gospel was one of the most insidious and dangerous traps that the enemy could have ever orchestrated against the people of God. Prospering is not wrong. It is taught in the scriptures, God wants us to prosper, but it was how it was taught and received that caused so many people to be ensnared by the devil. Many in the church were caught up in "materialism."

> The rich ruleth over the poor, and the borrower is servant to the lender. - Proverbs 22:7

What you failed to understand is that when you borrow, you are a servant or slave to that entity that you borrowed from, because of the conditions of the contract, and until it is paid off. If a life event happens such as sickness or unexpected expenses or job change, the contract is still in effect and the lenders expect to be paid. Interest rates can fluctuate due to one unintentional late payment.

When you borrow, your name and character is on the line with God. Psalms 37:31 states, "The wicked borroweth, and payeth not again: but the righteous sheweth mercy, and giveth". It does not matter the financial condition, God expects you to pay your debts.

The Religious Bait

It's sad to say but many churches and pastors have taught either directly or indirectly that the idea of being blessed and Godly is associated with material things, and neglected the teachings of financial responsibility as taught in the scriptures. The only aspect of the teaching that dealt with financial responsibility was, and still is the tithes and offerings, paid to the church. Those who have no concept of how of God and financial responsibility work, make sure these two things are paid by their members, but keep them in the snare of the enemy by teaching them prosperity based on material gain. Therefore, you pay the tithe and offering expecting big houses, lands, and cars. In your mind, even though you knew the scripture, subliminally, you associated gain with godliness.

Materialism

This is a form of "idolatry" because it is connected to a self-image that works in pride, and gaining the praise, and attention of men, becoming men pleasers.

In the church world, so many believers struggle to keep up an image of success rather than actually being successful. Some live above their means, or live one paycheck from disaster, yet, they possess the cars and houses; secretly struggling with high interest rates and long terms while saying to the public, "Look at how God has blessed me."

> Take heed, and beware of covetousness: for a man's life consisteth not in the abundance of the things, which he possesseth. - St. Luke 12:15

The Truth of the Matter

I can be cliché, and tell you to believe that God can restore all, speak the word over your situation, and watch God move. However, that will not help if the mindset towards God and your economic thinking does not change. That would leave you open to more satanic attacks of the same nature.

The truth is "you have simply assumed too much responsibility upon yourself." Because of your image complex and your desire for things, it is hard for you to let the material things go. This is not all your fault, because you hear it in church all the time, that "as a child of God, you suppose to have the best." So you take on jobs that take you away from church and ministry, you want to keep your things and maintain your image. The money is still not enough. Therefore, you work two or more jobs.

The deceitfulness of riches is thinking that materialism makes you look good and will bring you joy. The Satanic plan behind this is to get you to neglect your spiritual responsibilities. My brother, my sister; you have been snared. Remember you have to think strategically. You have to learn to let things go and get back to putting God first.

> Therefore, if God so clothe the grass of the field, which today is, and tomorrow is cast into the oven, shall he not much more clothe you, O ye of little faith? Therefore, take no thought, saying, What shall we eat? or, What shall we drink? or, Wherewithal shall we be clothed? For after all these things do the Gentiles seek :) for your heavenly Father knoweth that ye have need of all these things. But seek ye first the kingdom of God, and his righteousness; and all these things shall be added unto you. Take therefore no thought for the morrow: for the morrow shall take thought for the things of itself. Sufficient unto the day is the evil thereof. St Matthew 6:33-34

God is Your Source

The key to the lock that holds you as a prisoner of war in the economic trap, is putting God first and learning to be content. God is more concerned about your soul. He already knows what you have need of and has promised to supply "all of your needs, according to His riches and glory through Jesus Christ" *(Philippians 4:19)*. Let him restore it. God is your source through Jesus Christ.

It is through His blessings that our living for the Lord is accomplished, especially, if you are working in ministry. God does want you to have more than enough. It is his will for you to prosper.

The word prosper comes from the Greek "euodoo" which means "to succeed in reaching or to have a prosperous journey." Your journey is "life" and He wants you to enjoy it. In all that you do, it is Gods desire to prosper it, and give you good success. However, it has to be done right. God is your preserver.

> Thy righteousness is like the great mountains; thy judgments are a great deep: O Lord, thou preservest man and beast. How excellent is thy lovingkindness, O God! therefore the children of men put their trust under the shadow of thy wings. They shall be abundantly satisfied with the fatness of thy house; and thou shalt make them drink of the river of thy pleasures. For with thee is the fountain of life: in thy light shall we see light. - Psalms 36-6-9

When man places his trust in God; not the things, according to the scripture, "they shall be abundantly satisfied. There houses are blessed and they can enjoy the pleasures of prosperity in righteousness". This is living my friend, not struggling to hold onto things.

Be in Health.

What good is prospering without having good health? Health comes from "hugiaino" which means "sound health," that is to say health without flaws, defect, injury, or disease. Your body is the temple of Holy Ghost and He wants His dwelling fit, well maintained and operational. This does not mean you will never get sick or suffer a malady. Such events could be tests of faith to see if you will trust God, like in the story of Job and Apostle Paul, who suffered bodily sickness; described as a thorn in his flesh.

It is a known fact that even in secular circles; poverty contributes to poor health because the monetary means to attain medicines or medical care are not there. In some cases, the living conditions of the impoverished are inhumane. I firmly believe that if the soul is prospering and growing spiritually, one's physical health will spring forward also.

> My son, be attentive to my words; incline your ear to my sayings. Let them not escape from your sight; keep them within your heart. For they are life to those who find them, and healing to all their flesh. Proverbs 4:20-22

Beloved, your prosperity and health hinges on your spiritual growth and the proper application of the scriptures to your life. (Psalms 1:1-3 Blessed is the man that walketh not in the counsel of the ungodly, nor standeth in the way of sinners, nor sitteth in the seat of the scornful. But his delight is in the law of the Lord; and in his law doth he meditate day and night. And he shall be like a tree planted by the rivers of water, that bringeth forth his fruit in his season; his leaf also shall not wither; and whatsoever he doeth shall prosper). The true power to get wealth comes from God increasing you to be a resource, a blessing for those who need help.

Section II

Satan and His Demons

Chapter Six

The Fowler

The Fowler

A "fowler" is skilled in using various types of traps, nets, and snares for professionally catching birds. One method in particular is taming young birds, placing them in hidden cages and using their call to draw birds like them, to an area where a trap is set. Once the bird lands in the zone of the call, the fowler, who is concealed from its view, uses his arrows to kill the bird.

The word "fowler" comes from the Hebrew "yaquwsh" which means "snare" or "entangled." His occupation reveals his purpose. Satan is the fowler. His job is to get you spiritually entangled in troublesome situations where you think logically and decisively, forgetting the biblical teachings that could bring you deliverance.

Once you are in this state of confusion, your faith is diminished; he then springs the trap that prevents your growth progress in God. Now once the trap is sprung, the fowler has to be quick, so he uses his darts or arrows to pierce your spirit and bring you down. These darts represent the quick, strategic placement of wicked people, and the vices of his strategy to destroy your faith in God. This is why the scripture exhorts us to be prepared to defend against the work of the fowler.

> Wherefore take unto you the whole armour of God that ye may be able to withstand in the evil day, and having done all, to stand. Stand therefore, having your loins girt about with truth, and having on the breastplate of righteousness; And your feet shod

with the preparation of the gospel of peace; Above all, taking the shield of faith, wherewith ye shall be able to quench all the fiery darts of the wicked. And take the helmet of salvation, and the sword of the Spirit, which is the word of God: Praying always with all prayer and supplication in the Spirit, and watching thereunto with all perseverance and supplication for all saints; - Ephesians 6:13-18

Just the like the fowler avoids being seen by the birds that respond to the birdcall, Satan hides behind the scenes of your afflictions and temptations. In order to be successful, the hunter or fowler must be properly concealed by the environment. The best advantage would be to camouflage himself. *(Think about this)*. Camouflage helps the hunter blend into the surrounding weeds, stalks, or grassy landscape. Even the bow and arrow *(wicked people and vices used)* are camouflaged, so that when the hunter moves in while tracking the prey and preparing for the shot, the movements, even from above are not detected.

Satan is a wolf in sheep's clothing, a familiar spirit, or angel of light, camouflaged into the fellowship of believers who are weak in discernment. In many cases, he is hiding in plain sight. However, we as believers do not pay attention to the signs, because of our trusts in the brethren, friends, associates, atmosphere of praises, and excitement about God. We fail to watch in all things.

One of Satan's greatest accomplishments was to get people to believe that he does not exist. There are those who even profess to know God and Christ, but reject and refuse to believe in a real Satan. They have been deceived or have deceived themselves into believing that Satan is just a symbol of evil, and demons are the reflections of evil in the human heart.

Since his defeat and fall, he has taken on other names that describe his character. These names give us insight into who he really is. It is very important that we understand his names in order to recognize his schemes.

Who Is Satan?

His Character - His Motives

- **Serpent:** *(Genesis 3:1)* – "nachash" means "Snake or hiss or to whisper an enchantment". Satan speaks with a quality that attracts and holds the attention of the hearer. His words are also small and low in sound, but his words are not still and quiet. Satan's voice always imply motion and rush in order to take advantage of something but is also always in opposition to the will of God. Read (Genesis 3:4-7)

- **Accuser:** *(Revelation 12:10)* – "kategoreo" means "to accuse" or "accuse of a crime before a tribunal or publicly" (Job 1:9-11). Here, he is called "accuser" because he issued a complaint about the plans of God in the life of Job and his motivation for serving God as not being genuine.

- **Devil:** *(Ephesians 4:27)* – "diabolos" means "slanderer" or "traducer" which is to belittle, disparage, or vilify the reputation or worth of a person, place or idea. It would seem that "accuser" and "slanderer" implies the same thing, but they are not. The term "devil" implies the content of the accusation. He minimizes the worth of holy things, holy ideas, and holy people by defamation of their character and faith.

- **Dragon:** *(Revelation 12:9)* – "drakon" means a "fabulous type of serpent" which has the keen ability to see. The dragon or serpent possesses the ability to see sharp in or through the darkness. He recognizes the propensity to sin in the heart of a believer. He then capitalizes on the desire by designing temptations that draw the believer into his traps.

- **Adversary:** *(1 Peter 5:8)* – "antidikos" to display behavior that reduces the effectiveness, neutralizing or restraining power of an opposite force, influence or action. This describes the effectiveness of the satanic roar. When intruders enter a lions range, the lions send out a roar signaling other members of its pride to attack the intruder. The second purpose of the roar is during a hunt, the lion, when it's about to pounce upon its prey, roars, stunning the spirit of the prey, causing it to freeze. The prey is almost immediately fatigued, caught and devoured.

- **The Tempter:** *(St. Matthew 16:9)* "pierazo" signifies the type of testing that the enemy uses to find your strengths and weaknesses, so that he can formulate an attack against you. Usually these types of test are followed with trials that seek to break down the believer, causing them to appear unapproved and a failure before God.

His Status - His Dwelling

Prince of the Air

> Wherein in time past ye walked according to the course of this world, according to the prince of the power of the air, the spirit that now worketh in the children of disobedience:- Ephesians 2:2

Satan is the chief leader and founder of this worlds "social system" which operates in opposition to the will of God for the human race. His status as prince is not contradictory to his status as the "god of this world." The term "prince" refers to his status as the "chief principality" or evil spirit of this world system. The scripture also provides insight into his dwellings.

Satan is not in hell with a pitchfork, red in color, sitting on a throne while presiding over tormented souls in hell. With the exception of souls tormented in hell, this description is far from the truth. Satan's dwelling is in the atmosphere or the air. "Air" in Hebrew is "shameh" which refers to the visible expanse occupied by the clouds. He is not far from us. Always mimicking God, he wants to be nearby, listening and watching our every move. The "shameh" is not limited to earth's atmosphere. It also extends to include the expanse containing the stars known as space or the universe.

The God of this World

> In whom the god of this world hath blinded the minds of them, which believe not, lest the light of the glorious gospel of Christ, who is the image of God, should shine unto them. - 2 Corinthians 4:4

He is called a "god" here because of the world's acceptance of his policies over the word of God. Worshiping God involves obeying his commands and ideas which signifies a genuine love for Him *(St. John 14:15)*. The same rule applies to those who love darkness. Unknowingly, they love Satan, because they worship him through their deeds.

> The massive amounts of sinful activity that we are witnessing in these times are under his control, power, and influence. This is one reason why we are told to love not the world, neither the things that are in the world. To do so means that the love of God or for God is not in us (I John 2:15-16)

His godhood is permissive only because of man's will to disobey the will of God. When God's ideas and will is ignored and disobeyed, though the person may not acknowledge Satan as their God directly, the mere idea of choosing not to follow God's word makes them a follower of him. The only reason why a person would reject the gospel and the life God chose for them is that Satan has blinded their minds with unbelief.

Prince of Darkness

Darkness comes from the Greek "skotoo" or "skotos" which indicates obscurity and blindness of the intellect, which leads to the performance of moral and spiritual acts of evil.

> If we say that we have fellowship with him, and walk in darkness, we lie, and do not the truth: - 1 John 1:6

There are many who believe that they can still have fellowship with God through Christ, while still living a life of sin and immorality. These are those who have had their intellect or understanding corrupted by teachings that lack accountability, commitment, consecration and obedience to God's word.

> This then is the message, which we have heard of him, and declare unto you, that God is light, and in him is no darkness at all. If we say that we have fellowship with him, and walk in darkness, we lie, and do not the truth: But if we walk in the light, as he is in the light, we have fellowship one with another and the blood of Jesus Christ his Son cleanseth us from all sin. - 1 John 1:5-7

Satan, described as the "prince of darkness" indicates religious deception through the corruption of false teachings. These false teachings darken man's ability to understand the word of God as it relates to holy living. They fail at understanding the purpose of the work of the cross. As a result, ultimately, the "professed believer "is "alienated" from the life of God; claiming salvation and living in sin; spiritually ignorant to the fact that they are lost.

> This I say therefore, and testify in the Lord, that ye henceforth walk not as other Gentiles walk, in the vanity of their mind. Having the understanding darkened, being alienated from the life of God through the ignorance that is in them, because of the blindness of their heart: Who being past feeling have given themselves over unto lasciviousness, to work all uncleanness with greediness. But ye have not so learned Christ; If so be that ye have heard him, and have been taught by him, as the truth is in Jesus: That ye put off concerning the former conversation the old man, which is corrupt according to the deceitful lusts; And be renewed in the spirit of your mind; and that ye put on the new man, which after God is created in righteousness and true holiness.- Ephesians 4:17-24

His Occupation

Thief in Greek is "kleptes" or "Klepto" which implies a certainty of a stealth or secret attack or theft. Satan operates in secret, constantly watching his prey for any crack in a believer's character, that he could take advantage of with one of his devices. His methods are very insidious, harmless until the time comes to harm, inconspicuous until the time comes for him to be seen. The result is often exceedingly harmful to the life of the believer. He uses three methods to accomplish this goal.

- **Steal:** His method of stealing involves being secret, gradual and unexpected, but in a habitual manner. This process leads him to-
- **Kill:** This method is centered on depriving the believer's spiritual life.
- **Destroy:** Once the spiritual life is drained. His next move is ruin the believer's spiritual structure, foundation, and testimony beyond repair.

He is a Liar

Everything that Satan says is a lie. Nothing he says is truth. He is the complete opposite of Jesus Christ and God. The Greek for "Liar" is "pseustes" which means "falsifier." He takes the truth of God's word or anything that is truthful and devalues its credibility by planting seeds of doubt and unbelief in the mind, or he twists the truth into a more suitable belief that makes it easier to be entreated, producing a false conversion.

> Ye are of your father the devil, and the lusts of your father ye will do. He was a murderer from the beginning, and abode not in the truth, because there is no truth in him. When he speaketh a lie, he speaketh of his own: for he is a liar, and the father of it. - St. John 8:44

Every lie spoken, regardless of the source is from Satan. The scripture makes it plain that Satan is the "father of lies." The truth stops wherever a lie begins. Even a half-truth is still a lie. Half-truths are told with the intent to deceive.

Chapter Seven

The Trappers

What Are Demons?

> For we wrestle not against flesh and blood, but against principalities, against powers, against the rulers of the darkness of this world, against spiritual wickedness in high places. - Ephesians 6:12

There are certain traits or qualities manifested in a person's behavior that determines their character or spirit. These traits drive the mental and emotional capacity of an individual, manifesting a "personality." I am sure you have met a person who has responded to statements and questions in an unnecessarily sarcastic manner; using mean words and/or actions. Usually, you would say to yourself, "That person is "mean-spirited" or has a "mean-spirit." On the other hand, if you met a person who is nice, humble and treats you with respect, you would say that, "That person has a "kind-spirit" or is "sweet-spirited." Therefore, the traits manifested by the actions of the individual revealed their personality.

Demons are "spirits" that are identified by their personalities. The difference between the personalities of demons and humans is that humans can choose the make-up of their personalities. People can change. Demonic personalities are inherently wicked. They are always the same.

The word "demon" is not found in the New Testament scriptures of the King James Version of the bible. It is derived from the Latin translation "daemon" meaning "evil spirit" which is mentioned numerous times throughout the Old and New Testament scriptures. The basic definition of evil is morally bad or wicked. Morals are the principles within the standards that determine right and wrong living. Therefore, an evil spirit is an entity that can only operate totally opposite of all that is good and Godly.

Demonic personalities are manifested by their actions within you or towards you. Here is a list to consider:

- **The Lustful Spirit:** is a spirit that constantly drives a person into fulfilling all kinds of intense sexual desires.
- **The Jealous Spirit:** is a spirit that drives a person to become intolerant and hostile towards another person's possessions, successes, or advantages.
- **The Angry Spirit:** an angry spirit keeps a person constantly irritated, impatient and enraged, which can lead to manifestations of uncontrolled bursts of rage in actions or words.
- **The Spirit of Fear:** A fearful spirit keeps a person living in worry, alarm, and expectation of something dreadful. On the other hand, they live in cowardice, avoiding responsibility and thinking only of themselves in the face of danger and/or responsibilities, neglecting those that need him the most during times of trouble and toil.
- **The Bitter Spirit**: is a spirit that distresses the mind with constant thoughts of anger and resentment because of offense. It produces severe animosity towards the offender.
- **The Spirit of Infirmity:** This spirit causes mental, spiritual, and physical weakness. This spirit is especially present in sickness and disease. It weakens the will and mind of a person, crippling them mentally.
- **The Deaf and Dumb Spirit:** This spirit manifests in two ways: Rebellion in children and causes deafness and mutability. It will display outbursts of rage and tantrums, in the face of authority, because of its unwillingness to obey. Severe possessions can cause seizures and epileptic attacks.
- **The Spirit of Rejection:** This spirit attacks a person's self-esteem by making them feel worthless, pitiful, and hopeless.

It works especially through bullying, wearing down the victim through the torment of sadness, until it is able to possess. Once it possesses its victim, through the thoughts of worthlessness, loneliness, and hopelessness, it leads to suicide.

- **The Seducing Spirits:** The seducing spirit is the spirit of anti-Christ that works through fallen preachers who were once anointed by God. They seduce men into fellowships with a modern day gospel that does not involve, commitment and accountability nor does it promote holy living, but justifies sin and conformity to world views.

- **The Familiar Spirit:** A familiar spirit is a demon that possesses a person with a wicked disposition and motivates them to befriend you, while plotting to hinder your progress and destroy your credibility.

Demons are fallen angels. In Revelation 12:4, along with Satan, it was calculated that a third part of the angels were cast down to the earth. Some were reserved in chains and darkness until Judgment *(Jude 1:6, 2 Peter 2:4).*

Now dwelling in the atmosphere, under the command of Satan, they make up a highly, systemic and organized institution of demons with military rank and positions in this present world. These demons are the agents of Satan, working evil devices through people; directly opposing the work of God in your life.

The existence of demons challenges the faith of men who say they believe in God, but do not seek to live for him. According to James 2:19, demons also have faith:

> Thou believest that there is one God; thou doest well: the devils also believe, and tremble. - James 2:19

Their kind of faith does not operate in the areas of ministry. They cannot be saved and delivered from sin. The idea here is that they also believe in the existence of the almighty God, His Son, and the Holy Spirit. They are not atheists. In fact, they possess much more faith than atheists do. They tremble at the presence of the Lord, acknowledge Jesus as the Son, and pray to him:

And when he was come to the other side into the country of the Gergesenes, there met him two possessed with devils, coming out of the tombs, exceeding fierce, so that no man might pass by that way. And, behold, they cried out, saying, What have we to do with thee, Jesus, thou Son of God? (Recognition and acknowledgement) art thou come hither to torment us before the time? (Trembling at his presence) And there was a good way off from them an herd of many swine feeding. So the devils besought him, saying, If thou cast us out, suffer us to go away into the herd of swine. (Prayer) And he said unto them, Go. And when they were come out, they went into the herd of swine: and, behold, the whole herd of swine ran violently down a steep place into the sea, and perished in the waters. - St. Matthew 8:28-32

Demons possess the ability to reason and make decisions. This is something that you really need to consider. Reasoning involves, considering "why something is the way it is." If a problem is discovered, then a solution must be applied in order to solve the problem. Consider the words of our Lord.

When the unclean spirit is gone out of a man, he walketh through dry places, seeking rest, and findeth none. Then he saith, I will return into my house from whence I came out; and when he is come, he findeth it empty, swept, and garnished. Then goeth he, and taketh with himself seven other spirits more wicked than himself, and they enter in and dwell there: and the last state of that man is worse than the first. Even so shall it be also unto this wicked generation. - St. Matthew 12:43-45.

Here we find that a demon has been cast out of a person. The person has been cleansed of sin through faith in the word *(St. John 17:17 sanctify (cleanse) them through thy truth; your word is truth)*. It recognizes what has happened and "reasoned" that there is a problem. It cannot obtain residency again in the life of this person without help. Therefore, it comes up with a solution. It recruits several more spirits with stronger, wicked personalities than it-self, breaks the person down mentally, spiritually, takes up residency, and makes the life of that person more miserable than it was before he or she experienced salvation through the Lord Jesus Christ.

Demons are not figments of your imagination. You did not create them through the evil acts of the past. They are the motivators of all evils in the world. Demons are real entities that walk among you every day, every hour, every minute and second. They never sleep, always watching your every move, trying to sense your every thought. Constantly trying you, and testing you; figuring out ways to organize schemes that they can use to ensnare you into sin and bondage.

Demons in the Old Testament

Demons in the Old Testament were called, as they are known today as "Evil Spirits." In Judges 9:23-24, God sent an evil spirit among king Abimelech, and the men of Shechem in order to cause division. In Psalms 106:32-40, the Children of Israel mingled with pagan nations in idolatry and sacrificed their children to the demons of Canaan. In 1 Samuel 16:15-16 an evil spirit troubled King Saul after he disobeyed the command of God. Also an evil spirit provoked King Saul to jealousy and filled him with a desire to seek and kill young David *(1 Samuel 16:14-23)*.

Demons in the New Testament

The New Testament placed more emphasis on the work of demons when Jesus began his ministry. The works of darkness had to be made known. Some of the confrontations include a man possessed with a dumb spirit *(St. Matthew 9:32-33)*. A man in the synagogue had an unclean spirit *(St. Mark 1:23-27)*. Then there was the young boy who suffered seizures caused by a demon. *(St. Matthew 17:14-18)*. Jesus met a man out of the tombs who was possessed by the devil and a legion of demons *(St. Matthew 8:28-34)*. Note that these demons have some works that are similar and some that are different. However, they all accommodate each other's work. Paul mentions three types of demons.

Principalities

The word principality comes from the Greek "Arche" meaning chief or leader. Arche also indicates the beginning or origin of a thing. A chief *(principality)* demon named "Beelzebub" is mentioned in St. Matthew 12:24-27 in a discourse between Jesus and the Pharisees. In Daniel Chapter 10, the word prince is used to describe Michael, the Archangel as the appointed guardian over Israel *(verse 21)*. The angel that was delivering the message to Daniel met opposition with the prince of Persia and stated that when he returns, he will engage in another battle with the prince of Greece. The opposing princes *(verse 13, 20)* are chiefs or demonic principalities that rule over these territories on earth. This gives us more insight into their occupation.

Principalities are demonic forces that hold dominion over certain areas of earth, nations, states, cities, and territories. They are the high-ranking generals in Satan's army. They execute their plans through the lower level demon forces.

You must remember that Satan is the prince and ruler of the kingdoms of this world. Jesus himself confirms this: He has assigned certain demons to rule in specific areas, issuing orders to the powers, which are the authorities that execute his plans.

> Now is the judgment of this world: now shall the prince of this world be cast out. - St. John 12:31

Powers

"Powers" are the influential and enforcing demons that execute the laws of the principal demons in their assigned areas. Consider them as the state officials governing their assigned territories. The Greek for "powers" is "exousia" which means privilege or force. This is the power to take over by privilege granted, forcing one into subjection, and assuring that the law of land, which is unrighteousness, is enforced.

They exercise the power of influence and persuasion; forcing men to do things that they would not normally do, leading them into spiritual enslavement. Usually, there influence can be heard in music, seen in movies, and in literature. They motivate men to commit wicked acts and operate through false teachers; corrupting the influence of the gospel so that their influence can remain dominant in the world. Consider the event in the city Ephesus:

> Many of them also which used curious arts brought their books together, and burned them before all men: and they counted the price of them, and found it fifty thousand pieces of silver. - Acts 19:19

After the people of Ephesus witnessed the humiliation of the powerless vagabond Jews, the people, out of fear, confessed their deeds and burned their books of curious arts, which taught "witchcraft."

Ephesus was a city full of people that were demon possessed. The principality over the city orchestrated the religious order using demons of witchcraft, which held the city captive through their worship of idols.

One idol in particular was a pagan goddess named "Diana," which was the most prominent idol god worshipped in Ephesus. The influence that this spirit had over the city of Ephesus brought riches to the craftsmen that created idols for Diana and her worshippers, but not without the cost of demon possession. The word was spread through Paul's preaching and miracles. Confirming his ministry the more, the humiliating incident of the seven sons of Sceva, boosted the word of God to grow more mightily, disrupting the influence of the demon powers.

A silversmith name Demetrius, who had made a fortune from the worship of Diana; stirred the people by testifying to other silversmiths about the message of the Apostle Paul. He stated that he preached, saying that "there were no gods made with hands, and how many people turned away from the worship of these gods and that the temple of the goddess Diana and everything about her should be despised". The main motivation behind Demetrius testimony was that their craft of creating false idol images and silver shrines was in danger of losing business and closing down. This caused an uproar. Which could have cost Apostle Paul his life. The people were under the influence of the pagan territorial demons that demanded worship of Diana and other false gods *(demons)* at Ephesus.

The entire city was engulfed in confusion and wrath behind Demetrius testimony. Understand the demonic influence over the people. When the people rushed Paul's companions into a theatre, there were all sorts of screams, crying out against the men. Some were screaming out against the men of Macedonia, not knowing why they were screaming.

The people of Ephesus were influenced by demonic powers, almost to the point of killing anyone who opposed Diana and her temple. Their minds were completely blinded from the gospel of Jesus Christ, even after witnessing the word of God being confirmed through miracles.

> But, if our gospel be hid, it is hid to them that are lost: In whom the god of this world hath blinded the minds of them which believe not, lest the light of the glorious gospel of Christ, who is the image of God, should shine unto them.- 2 Corinthians 4:3-4

The powers that ruled this area demanded that only the doctrine of Diana and the worship of her and other false deities were enforced. Demetrius was the counter strategy against the power of the Kingdom of God. These demons exercised their power over an entire city through the testimony of one man.

The Rulers of the Darkness

The rulers of the darkness are the mastering demons, which will blind your mind from the liberty that is found in the word of God. They will hide the truth through false teachings, deception, unbelief and doubt; leading you into spiritual servitude. Though these are the lower level demons, they are specific in their office and are recognized by the actions that they will lead you to perform.

Apostle Paul goes on to explain to the Ephesian church that these rulers of the darkness are the agents of all moral depravity in this world system. Because men love darkness *(evil)* more than light *(righteousness),* they have gained dominion over areas where those who love darkness dwell.

> And this is the condemnation, that light is come into the world, and men loved darkness rather than light, because their deeds were evil. For every one that doeth evil hateth the light, neither cometh to the light, lest his deeds should be reproved. - St. John 3:19-20

They Blind You To The Truth

> Then shalt thou understand righteousness, and judgment, And equity; yea, every good path. When wisdom entereth into thine heart, And knowledge is pleasant unto thy soul; Discretion shall preserve thee, Understanding shall keep thee: To deliver thee from the way of the evil man, From the man that speaketh froward things; Who leave the paths of uprightness, To walk in the ways of darkness; -Proverbs 2:11-13

Speaking froward things are "words "that promote disobedience and rebellion, they encourage unrighteous living and actions. Darkness describes the words and actions that are rebellious, froward, and deceitful, blinding you to the truth and consequences of your actions.

Solomon makes a clear statement that wisdom is the result of understanding the knowledge of righteousness and judgment, which places you on a good path. The key term here is "judgment," which is having the mental capacity to distinguish between bad and good relationships, situations, and circumstances, using the knowledge of righteousness, enabling you to discern the words that would lead you to believe that you are making the right decision or the wrong one.

All men, before coming into the knowledge of Jesus Christ, walked in and enjoyed the pleasures of sin until the time came when they realized the price that had to be paid for enjoying those pleasures. Sin blinds you with darkness, false knowledge, and false wisdom that walk you into the snares of sin.

> Then Jesus said unto them, Yet a little while is the light with you. Walk while ye have the light, lest darkness come upon you: for he that walketh in darkness knoweth not whither he goeth. - St. John 12:35

Understand that the bible teaches that the word of God is a lamp and a light that guides the directions of the believer, helping him to avoid the tragedies of making the wrong decisions. Darkness or evil instruction covers that pathway that leads the follower down a path of destruction that is unbeknown to him. *(Psalms 119:105 - Thy word is a lamp unto my feet, and a light unto my path.)*. Therefore, the ultimate purpose of the rulers of darkness is to cause those who would and are following Jesus Christ to turn away from the truth of God's word. Once these demons blind you to the truth of your actions; their personalities become prevalent through wicked acts.

Spiritual Wickedness

Wickedness in the Greek is "poneria" or "poneros" which represents an active form of evil or influence, emanating from a malicious and depraved disposition toward yourself or another person. This type of wickedness causes extensive labor, toil, pain, and sorrow in your life, which results in living below divine expectations. Examples of spiritual wickedness are:

- Murder
- Deceit
- Lust
- Pride
- Lies
- Fear
- Jealousy

- Self-Righteousness
- Gluttony
- Greed
- Slothfulness
- Wrath
- Vanity

These are some of the evil personalities manifested by the rulers of the darkness. This is important to know, because it will help you to understand why Christian warfare is not against flesh and blood. However, it is against the work of Satan and demons in the hearts of men. This brings us to the high places.

High Places

Now we must understand the meaning of the high place. It does refer to demon forces operating in high positions of authority. However, the high place is somewhere more significant. It is the human spirit. In the Old Testament, a high place was an elevated site located on a hill, in a valley or at the top of a mountain; containing an altar and symbols, where pagans worshipped and sacrificed to false gods.

For he built up again the high places which Hezekiah his father had destroyed; and he reared up altars for Baal, and made a grove, as did Ahab king of Israel; and worshipped all the host of heaven, and served them. - 2 Kings 21:3

Worship is "shachah" which means reverence, devotion, and allegiance pledged to a god. It involves bowing down to someone in an act of submission. "Sacrifice" implies "the offering of a life upon an altar." These alters no longer exist, except in the hearts of men, where worship takes place.

The high place is the unregenerated human heart of man; therefore, they are prone to be used by demonic forces against you in thought, words, and deeds. This is why you should do all according to the will of God to guard your spirits.

> Keep thy heart with all diligence; for out of it are the issues of life. Put away from thee a froward mouth, and perverse lips put far from thee. Let thine eyes look right on, and let thine eyelids look straight before thee. Ponder the path of thy feet, and let all thy ways be established. Turn not to the right hand nor to the left: remove thy foot from evil-. Proverbs 4:23-27.

Chapter Eight

The Spirit of Rejection

The need for acceptance by others is a subtle emotion that drives you from birth to connect with other people. During a child's growth period, the child seeks acceptance and affirmation from its parents. When the child does something artistic, with excitement, the child seeks the parent's approval by showing them their creation.

This attitude follows them to the classroom. A new atmosphere with those who are of the same age and likeness brings new challenges. Unknown to the child, they begin to suffer anxiety. They experience the tension of being left alone without mommy or daddy. The idea of sitting at a table with another child that they have never seen before can bring about withdrawal and/or aggression.

If a child or group of children does not want to play with the child, this may drive the child to seclusion. The rejecting party of children may not have a specific reason for rejecting another child; it is just part of the human experience.

The need for acceptance is also experienced when entering the workforce. It starts at the job interview. Anxiety can set in because you are hoping to do well, by answering every interview question properly. If you are hired, you look to be accepted by your fellow co-workers. You start to mingle, let them instruct you on things you may already know. You may tolerate ridicule, when mistakes are made in your work, because you want to fit in. When you meet someone you like and want to spend time with, you dress yourself nicely, adjust your character, and choose your words wisely, when speaking, hoping to gain the person's admiration. However, when that need of acceptance is not met, it can throw you off balance, spiritually, emotionally, or mentally.

What is Rejection?

Rejection is a human experience that every human being has and will experience at some point in their life. You may not get the opportunity to interview with a recruiter because they may deem your skills as insufficient. There will be people who will not accept you in their circles because they feel you're not the type to hang out with, and the request to start a relationship with someone you like may be declined. Rejection is a part of life.

When an evil spirit is involved, rejection is a deliberate and intentionally hostile with the intent to make you feel worthless, useless, and unsupported. This demonic influence of rejection attacks your identity and self-worth.

Demonic rejection occurs when one is cast away, refused, or put aside as worthless or useless. It makes you believe that you are who are you are based on how other people accept you. It works side by side with the spirit of fear or cowardice.

Satan's Opportunity

Rejection itself is not evil. It helps us to see where we need to adjust characteristics or qualifications in order to join certain groups that require those adjustments. Satan and his demons take advantage of the idea of rejection and use it as a means to attack your mind, identity, and self-worth. Because of the human need to belong, when rejection occurs, Satan bombards the mind with intrusive thoughts that breed emotions of offense, low-esteem, feeling unloved, unwanted and fear. For instance, Just the mere act of defriending a person on Facebook can be considered an offensive move against the rejected. Because it sends the signal that you are negative in some kind of way, what you have to say is not important or you do not meet that person's criteria of what a friend should be.

It is a normal response to feel saddened if you tried to join an organization or group and realized you have been denied entrance. However, you give place to the devil when you somber over it.

Sombering is seen as weakness, and it attracts demons like bees to honey, opening doors to many snares.

Real Rejection

There are two types of rejection. The first is "real rejection" This form of rejection operates by treating you as a foreign tissue attached to a new body. The immune system of the body constantly attacks the foreign until it is weak, fragile, and soon detached.

Children will internalize their depression, when suffering from this spirit, especially if they are bullied. The spirit of rejection causes bullying. This causes low self-esteem and as a result, they will act out aggressively or go into seclusion.

In your walk with Christ, you cannot assume that everyone in your life will accept you. Not everyone in church is saved. You may suffer rejection from some of these brethren. In the workplace, there are conspirators, toxic and power hungry individuals that breed trouble and negativity. There could be numerous reasons for people to reject you. Sometimes, your very presence on a new job or in a new family will cause you to be rejected.

In some cases, rejection may not be motivated by evil. Sometimes people are not compatible. A woman may be good friends with a man, and cannot see herself in an intimate relationship with him. Some people, you may find friendly, but the lack of common interests may not hold the relationship together. There is no evil here. In these cases, it becomes a matter of how you respond.

Church Rejection

You will encounter people in fellowships who will refuse to believe that your conversion is real and they will reject you. Some may feel like you may not meet their standard of what the bible and holy living is all about and they will reject you.

In abusive ministries, the spirit of rejection will sometimes emanate from leadership. The voice of this spirit can be heard in the sermons. Instead of true critique and constructive criticism, the words are insulting and character destroying.

The spirit of rejection will manifest itself in favoritism. Favoritism is unfair partiality or fair treatment toward another person at the expense of someone else. It operates more prevalent in smaller fellowships, causing confusion in various church offices. If your possessions or financial contributions are not as substantial as someone else is, or your dress style may not be as good, you may not be allowed to operate in your church freely as others. You may find your condition as a topic of many messages; you may be rejected from singing lead in the choir and so forth. A clear sign of rejection is when you're constantly being pushed to the back. Look at what St. James says about this:

> My brethren, have not the faith of our Lord Jesus Christ, the Lord of glory, with respect of persons. For if there come unto your assembly a man with a gold ring, in goodly apparel, and there come in also a poor man in vile raiment; And ye have respect to him that weareth the gay clothing, and say unto him, Sit thou here in a good place; and say to the poor, Stand thou there, or sit here under my footstool: Are ye not then partial in yourselves, and are become judges of evil thoughts? Hearken, my beloved brethren, Hath not God chosen the poor of this world rich in faith, and heirs of the kingdom which he hath promised to them that love him? But ye have despised the poor. Do not rich men oppress you, and draw you before the judgment seats? Do not they blaspheme that worthy name by the which ye are called?If ye fulfil the royal law according to the scripture, Thou shalt love thy neighbour as thyself, ye do well: But if ye have respect to persons, ye commit sin, and are convinced of the law as transgressors.-St. James 2:1-9

Workplace Rejection

In the workplace, you will encounter people who may not want to work with you, or want to control you. In order to control you, your work is compared to another employees work and is merely complimented or rejected, whereas the other worker, whose work is of the same quality, is rewarded. If you feel a desire to respond by seeking the manager's merit or favor, after being unequally criticized, the spirit of rejection is working on you.

Workplace rejection is also manifested through managers and employees who divide the workforce through competition and pitting co-workers against one another.

People that allow this spirit to work in them will bring you turmoil; constantly causing issues in the workplace and at the same time, make petty complaints about you.

Relationship Rejection

You may have entered a relationship, where your future spouse's family is rejecting you, simply because they think you are not good enough. Here are a few signs that prove when the spirit of rejection is at work:

- You're constantly snubbed or pushed away.
- You're ignored.
- You're constantly talked about.
- You're not included in meetings.
- In your presence, the person is mostly silent.
- The person cannot hold a conversation with you.
- You catch the rejecter frowning at you.
- If you walk towards the person, they turn away from you.
- They ask prying or humiliating question about you.

Rejection In Marriage

The spirit of rejection in marriage is manifested when the spouse is denied communication. The rejecting spouse ignores requests to talk, ignores your intimate needs and concerns. The rejecting spouse may speak harsh and sometimes, insulting words that could negatively affect your confidence.

The spirit of rejection after a divorce can devastate a former spouse's emotions. They can feel less attractive and fall into fear of ever getting involved in another relationship. The rejected spouse can fall into heavy depression, insecurity, anger and take on a victimized character, where they seek nothing but pity.

These actions are baits. How you feel about yourself will determine your response. How you respond can set off the trap.

Suffering such attitudes can lead you to create more chaos in your life. They can lead you to:

- Create a personality in order to fit in.
- Join groups and organizations in order to please the rejecting party.
- Taking on a feeling of self-worthlessness and insecurity.
- Feel like you don't fit in, so you leave your church, quit your job, and separate. yourself from even those who care about you.

When you experience real rejection, you can become intellectually burdened with the negative thoughts of how you were treated. Satan then hampers your performance in the workplace, home, and/or church life; transforming you into an emotional wreck. That leads me to discuss the next form of rejection.

Imagined Rejection

Imagined rejection is the second form that is a result of the fear of rejection or the result of real rejection. This facet of rejection takes place in the mind. Real rejection can cause low self-esteem, whereas imagined rejection is the manifested result of low self-esteem. Imagined rejection causes high anxiety and stress. Imagined rejection produces paranoia. It causes its victim to believe that people dislike or hate them. The preconceived ideas of such thoughts are again, rising from how you feel about yourself. In either case, how you view yourself will determine your response. Imagined rejection reveals these characteristics:

- Loneliness and anti-sociability; fearing that people will not receive you in their circles.
- Defensive and sensitive to constructive criticism.
- Living on the offense.
- Rejecting others as to avoid rejection first.
- Paranoia.
- Seeking the praise of others or by wanting to be noticed by going the extra mile all the time.

Regardless of the form of rejection, you may be suffering; it leads you to live a life of falsehood, which will inevitably lead you down a path of severe disappointments and other satanic snares. Some of these snares are unforgiveness, jealousy bitterness, and self-condemnation.

Negative Self-Talk

Negative self-talk is the inner voice that you use to communicate how you feel about yourself and situations. Negative self-talk, can start with voices in your head that speak less of your character, qualifications, and identity. Here are some are examples of thoughts:

Intelligence

- I can't believe I was that stupid.
- Maybe I am not that smart as others.
- I am not qualified. I deserve to be dropped.
- I can't meet the standards, so maybe I should try something else.
- I am failure.

Emotions

- I am so angry right now .
- It's all my fault.
- I am so depressed.
- I'm so stupid.
- I am not good enough.
- I'm worthless .

Physical Attacks

- I don't look the part.
- I don't look as good as they do.
- I am ashamed of myself.

The moment you start giving into these thoughts, you allow yourself to enter into the trap of being controlled and manipulated by the rejecting party. This can lead to many evils. You fall under their control based on a few negative factors:

- You produce a negative self-image of yourself.
- You over generalize things.
- You dwell only on the negatives of your life.

- You allow feelings of guilt to permeate your spirit.
- You blame yourself or the one who caused your pain. *(I am such a loser; he or she has ruined my life.)*
- You adjust yourself to meet their standards so that you can be accepted *(The standards determine whether it is right or wrong).*

The more negative you are, the more your spirit will deteriorate into other negative emotions. Your views and perceptions become more and more distorted, and your actions more irrational. Even afterwards, you can still be rejected. Why? You can never please men.

All negative self-talk deals with the satanic "ifs" that Satan presented to Jesus before he started his earthly ministry. These "ifs" challenged his divinity, so they will challenge your identity.

> And when he had fasted forty days and forty nights, he was afterward an hungred. And when the tempter came to him, he said, If thou be the Son of God, command that these stones be made bread. But he answered and said, It is written, Man shall not live by bread alone, but by every word that proceedeth out of the mouth of God. Then the devil taketh him up into the holy city, and setteth him on a pinnacle of the temple, And saith unto him, If thou be the Son of God, cast thyself down: for it is written, He shall give his angels charge concerning thee: and in their hands they shall bear thee up, lest at any time thou dash thy foot against a stone. Jesus said unto him, It is written again, Thou shalt not tempt the Lord thy God. Again, the devil taketh him up into an exceeding high mountain, and sheweth him all the kingdoms of the world, and the glory of them. And saith unto him, All these things will I give thee, if thou wilt fall down and worship me. Then saith Jesus unto him, Get thee hence, Satan: for it is written, Thou shalt worship the Lord thy God, and him only shalt thou serve. - St. Matthew 4:2-10

The first two temptations dealt with Satan tempting him to prove who he was. When the tempter asked him to turn the stones to bread, he was appealing to his human need, the need to eat. This is similar to our need to fit in or to be accepted by a person or group. If Jesus had turned the stones to bread, he would have also been tempted to eat. The tempter would have certainly capitalized on that opportunity and every opportunity that followed. The same rule applies to the believer who needs to be accepted. If the believer compromises just one time to satisfy the need to fit in, he will constantly be tempted to bend even more to maintain that satisfaction.

Next, he tempts him to cast himself down, using the scriptures as a means to get him to prove himself. Because he used the scriptures, obviously this religious temptation appeals to his beliefs. In a church setting, you will come across those who will use the scriptures as a means of evaluation for you to be accepted into a fold that is primarily based on doctrines designed by men. They will use the idea of unquestionable service and a hard commitment of works to prove that your service is genuine.

The temptations were snares, designed to get Jesus to sin in pleasing man for the sake of acceptance. The last temptation dealt with Jesus giving up all that he knew of himself, God and righteousness and follow Satan. The same is how the spirit of rejection will snare your soul.

All the negative self-talk will lead you down a road where you constantly seek the approval of men, lowering yourself to meet their standards of who you should be, and neglecting who and what God made you to be through His grace. Jesus knew who he was. Your victory in dealing with this spirit will require you to do the same. Not knowing who you are and what God has made you to be, will lead to you the next phase.

Self-Condemnation

Condemnation comes from "katakrima" which is Greek for "a sentence or judgment pronounced with a suggestion of punishment without forgiveness." It is connected to "katakrino" which means to "condemn with judgment or pass sentence upon someone for a crime." Self-condemnation sets in when you accept the negative thoughts of worthlessness and hopelessness that comes from being rejected, and believing that you deserve less or are non-deserving. It is the final step before spiritual suicide.

Spiritual suicide is the last phase of self-condemnation. This is where Satan suggests thoughts of backsliding away from God. He suggests thoughts such as "you will never live up to the standards that God is calling for' or "God will not accept you, because you are unworthy."

These are the thoughts that drive you to leave your church, your job, your family and commitments that would help you live a vibrant life in Jesus Christ. In order to overcome self-condemnation is to realize that in Christ Jesus, there is no condemnation *(Romans 8:1)*.

In order to overcome self-condemnation, you have to walk in the spirit of God. Even if you have failed in a task before those who have rejected you, Understand, that all have fallen short of Glory of God.

In Jesus Christ, you have been made free and are no longer, held accountable for your past sins. It is the life without Christ, which brings misery and bondage. This is the work of rejection. Through negative thinking, the life of Christ can be drained.

Think Strategically

> There is therefore now no condemnation to them, which are in Christ Jesus, who walk not after the flesh, but after the Spirit. For the law of the Spirit of life in Christ Jesus hath made me free from the law of sin and death. - Romans 8:1

One of the main reasons why Jesus Christ gained the victory over the snares of temptations in the wilderness was because he knew who he was and he knew his purpose.

> And it came to pass, that after three days they found him in the temple, sitting in the midst of the doctors, both hearing them, and asking them questions. And all that heard him were astonished at his understanding and answers. And when they saw him, they were amazed: and his mother said unto him, Son, why hast thou thus dealt with us? behold, thy father and I have sought thee sorrowing. And he said unto them, How is it that ye sought me? wist ye not that I must be about my Father's business? And they understood not the saying which he spake unto them. And he went down with them, and came to Nazareth, and was subject unto them: but his mother kept all these sayings in her heart. And Jesus increased in wisdom and stature, and in favour with God and man. - St. Luke 2:46-52.

Jesus, as a child was found among doctors and lawyers, asking questions and gaining understanding of laws and public concerns, preparing himself for his ministry. His response to Mary saying, "That he must be about his Fathers business," indicates that he knew he was and the purpose for which he came. He did not need another's' merit, nor his parents confirmation of his identity. Knowing this caused him to grow in the favour of God and in the favour of men.

When you accepted Jesus as your Lord and savior, you must recognize who you are in Christ. You must know your identity. When you recognize your identity in Jesus Christ, the need to be accepted by men is destroyed and the snare is rendered ineffective. The only standards you need to meet are those outlined in the word of God. These standards will empower you to do your work as unto the Lord, influencing the favour of men in your life.

You are more than a just an old sinner that has received forgiveness of sins. You were then and are loved by God. Even when you were His enemy:

> But God commendeth his love toward us, in that, while we were yet sinners, Christ died for us. - Romans 5:8

You are not justified by works. You are saved through faith in Jesus Christ. Christ justified you. He has rendered you innocent as if you had never sinned *(Galatians 2:16)*. You are now a spiritual house of God, a holy priesthood, designed to send up spiritual sacrifices of praise and glory in worship to God. You have direct access to God, through Jesus Christ. This is fulfilled through your willingness to obey His commands.

You are part of a holy nation, set apart from a wicked world system, presenting yourself as an instrument of righteousness. You are peculiar, you are "periousios" meaning special or "Gods own possession" purchased through the blood of Jesus Christ.

> Wherefore also it is contained in the scripture, Behold, I lay in Sion a chief corner stone, elect, precious: and he that believeth on him shall not be confounded. Unto you therefore which believe he is precious: but unto them, which be disobedient, the stone,

which the builders disallowed, the same is made the head of the corner, And a stone of stumbling, and a rock of offence, even to them which stumble at the word, being disobedient: whereunto also they were appointed. But ye are a chosen generation, a royal priesthood, an holy nation, a peculiar people; that ye should shew forth the praises of him who hath called you out of darkness into his marvellous light; Which in time past were not a people, but are now the people of God: which had not obtained mercy, but now have obtained mercy. Dearly beloved, I beseech you as strangers and pilgrims, abstain from fleshly lusts, which war against the soul; Having your conversation honest among the Gentiles: that, whereas they speak against you as evildoers, they may by your good works, which they shall behold, glorify God in the day of visitation.- 1 Peter 2:6-12

Just as Jesus Christ became a stumbling stone to the chief priests, you are a lively stone rejected by those who may not be in the faith. Your conversion to true faith is a testament to how a true Christian should live. Therefore, you are hated.

He came unto his own, and his own received him not. - St. John 1:11

However, his rejection did not stop him from fulfilling his purpose. Jesus knew he was and knew what he came to do. He did not need the validation of any man in order to pursue his purpose. You have to know who you are in Christ. The word of God is the only validation you need and is the only validation you should seek. You will find it in the love of God. Realize that you have been adopted into the family of God and your suffering identifies with His righteous family.

And if children, then heirs; heirs of God, and joint-heirs with Christ; if so be that we suffer with him, that we may be also glorified together.- Romans 8:17

Realize how blessed you are and what Christ has done for you on the cross and when you accepted him as savior.

As far as the east is from the west, so far hath he removed our transgressions from us. - Psalms 103:12

You have to accept the fact that God loves you, and He proved it by giving up His only begotten son to be crucified, so that you can have a purpose in life. In addition, you have to love yourself. Realize that you are who God made you to be and that everything he created was good. Purge your mind by yielding your ways to God and he will establish your thoughts. Think strategically and escape the snare of rejection.

Chapter Nine

The Spirit of Fear

The Spirit of Fear

Fear is a normal emotional and sub-conscious mechanism, which triggers survival instincts, as a response to actual threats of danger. In some situations, fear is beneficial. It can motivate you to protect your loved ones and yourself from danger. Webster defines "fear" as being afraid or being apprehensive which means' "having suspicion or fear, especially of future harm of evil."

There is a difference between healthy fears and demonic fears. In order to recognize the evil spirit of fear we have to put "fear" in general, in its proper perspective.

Healthy Fear

I can remember a time, during my childhood, at my grandmother's house, my uncle was in the kitchen preparing what I thought was breakfast. Letting curiosity get the best of me, I grabbed the handle of a pot that was on the stove, thinking that it was a pot of grits. Suddenly, but too late, I could hear my uncle scream, "BOY, NO!" Out of that, pot, poured boiling hot water, spilling all of over my chest. The last events I can remember is riding in the car with some family members to the emergency room, laying on a table and a doctor removing burned skin from my chest. In my sub-conscious, I knew, never again to approach stoves and pots in the manner, in which I did at first, out of fear of the previous event. This is a healthy fear. It helps to avoid harm.

If a child reaches for and/or touches a stove, they can detect the heat with their little finger tips and withdraw. With a stern and loving tone, mother will say the words "hot. Do not touch!" When they enter the kitchen again and see the stove, they will repeat the words hot, while pointing. Subconsciously, the child fears the harm the stove will bring based on his remembrance of mommy's words.

Healthy fears in the face of danger will cause you to take action. If you see a pack of dogs running towards you, foaming and barking wildly, your initial reaction would be to run and escape the pack. Not only is that a healthy fear, it is also good common sense. A healthy fear will cause you to go to the doctor when you detect that something in your body is not functioning properly. A healthy fear will grow from actual dangers and will subside when the threat is no more.

Unhealthy fears

These types of fears are demonically motivated due to the exaggeration of the threat that never seems to subside. In addition, these threats, if any, present little to no danger at all. They seem threatening because the demon of fear magnifies the threat. When Satan magnifies a threat, phobias are formed. Such are:

- Fear of water
- Fears of animals
- Fear of spiders
- Fear of enclosed places
- Fear of storms
- Fear of the dark

An unhealthy fear will cloud your judgment and cause you to act without thinking. The spirit of fear spoken of in scripture is when a person's mental disposition is shaken, flawed, or decayed, due to threats that present little to no danger at all. Imagined threats are formed from ignorance; fearing the unknown. These imagined threats distract you from what is real and purposeful. They stop you from moving forward and getting on with your life.

Fear is like a lions roar to its prey. It sounds off to warn the prey of its presence, while paralyzing it, allowing it enough time to pounce and devour.

For God hath not given us the spirit of fear; but of power, and of love, and of a sound mind. - 2 Timothy 1:7

In this verse, the Greek term for "fear" is "deilia" which means cowardice, unmanliness, or timidity. The spirit of fear will strip you of your assurance of salvation, producing doubt and discouragement, causing you to remain in a constant state of alarm. You will find yourself easily disturbed with no confidence in God and his word. Before your enemies, the spirit of fear will cause you to walk with your head down, pounding you with intrusive thoughts of shyness, rejection, and paranoia. It will make you spineless, always bowing down to trial and tribulation. You will become fainthearted. Everything discourages you and excels itself above your faith, removing your ability to assert yourself in the power of God.

Fear is the key that opens doors to other demonic attacks and trappings. What makes fear tormenting is that it paralyzes you when you are face to face with your problems. You cannot react, you cannot move. Like a prey freezes at the roar of a lion, so you freeze at the effects of fear and are consumed in the trap.

The trap of fear places you on spiritual lock down. You become emotionally distressed, paranoid, easily offended and angry; and sometimes angry over things that has not happened yet. The result is not being able to grab a hold on life's helm and move forward.

Cowardice

A "coward" in the face of danger will exercise flawed judgment by thinking of his own well-being, neglect to do what is right, and flee, even if it means abandoning those that are in need of his help.

If you're a man, fear will drain your manliness. If you're a woman, it will drain your strength and courage. "Unmanliness" is displaying characteristics that are not becoming of a man. This demon force weakens your character to the point of being feminine, soft, or womanish. Now this is not an insult to women, it refers to the desire of the woman who puts her trust in her man to protect her. Instead of you facing your fear and handling the difficulty, you seek to be protected as the woman seeks protection from her husband. The spirit of fear in the life of a man will strip him of his masculinity causing him to be excessively soft, delicate and self-indulgent in the face of danger, running from responsibility in difficult times, even it means compromising his faith for ease.

Cowardice creates timidity. In the face of people, you become tense and bashful, fearing interaction. It will cause you to withdraw, eating away at your self-confidence, boldness, and determination. This is how social phobias are formed. Fear, like rejection, causes you think what others think about you or have to say about you.

This spirit diminishes a person's mental and moral strength to engage the enemy and persevere in a difficult battle. There are three types of fear or cowardly characteristics:

- **Physical Fear:** This is when the will of God or your situation requires your physical engagement, but you remain frozen or inactive in fear of hardship and difficulties neglecting your spiritual and natural responsibilities.
- **Moral Fear:** You choose not to do the right thing morally in fear of persecution, rejection, or loss. This involves a compromise of holy standards and behaviors in order to be accepted by a person or a group.
- **Spiritual Fear:** This involves your emotions and imaginations. These types of fears form phobias and terrors of things that pose very little threat, they can be imagined and pose no threat at all. It is all in the mind.
- **Moral Fear:** A moral fear will cause a person to side with the majority in fear of confrontation in order to abide in peace with the majority, even if the majority is wrong. This demon force will remove your spiritual spine to stand up for what you believe in.

In St. John 12:42-44, many of the chief priests believed in Jesus Christ, but would not confess a faith in him and accept him as Lord. If they sided with Jesus Christ, the Pharisees would have denounced them publicly as heretics, and excommunicate them out of the synagogue. This would have caused a rebuttal and persecution from the public who followed and heeded the teachings of the Pharisees. They found it to be beneficial to them to earn the praises of men than to endure persecution for following Jesus Christ, even at the cost of denying that he was the messiah.

In St. Matthew 26:69-75, Peter, exercised this form of fear in order to avoid scandal and persecution when Jesus stood before Caiaphas and the Sanhedrin. The people questioned him three times, if he knew whom Jesus was and was he with him. Each time he denied knowing the Lord and the third denial was with cursing.

Whenever you find yourself in a position, where you feel tempted to compromise your beliefs in Christ or your morals for the sake of the majority, in order to feel accepted, loved, avoid ridicule and persecution for your stand, the spirit of fear is working on you.

An example of such cowardice is notable in the many modern day religious leaders who are conforming to tolerate homosexuality as a way of life, because of the secular majority and the fear of persecution. Those who speak against the act, by speaking the truth of God's word, are demonized by the media and the LGBT community. However, some, when they are asked if homosexuality is a sin, the either dally around the answer or come up with some lame justification by purposely misinterpreting the scripture.

The Cause of Moral Fear

If you find yourself compromising your faith in Jesus Christ and your standards for living, your compromise is evidence to the fact that you have not denied yourself. Your desire is after this worlds system and the things it has to offer.

As a Christian, you cannot compromise your holy standards in order to move forward in life and yet be effective in the kingdom of God and pleasing in the eyes of God. The devil knows this. Moreover, in these times of political correctness, the pressure to be different, possessing integrity and honesty in business, relationships, and ministry is more challenging than ever before. Therefore, many are now compromising their faith in Christ for the status quo. Heed the words of our Lord concerning moral fear and compromise:

> And when he had called the people unto him with his disciples also, he said unto them, Whosoever will come after me, let him deny himself, and take up his cross, and follow me. For whosoever will save his life shall lose it; but whosoever shall lose his life for my sake and the gospel's, the same shall save it. For what shall it profit a man, if he shall gain the whole world,

and lose his own soul? Or what shall a man give in exchange for his soul? Whosoever therefore shall be ashamed of me and of my words in this adulterous and sinful generation; of him also shall the Son of man be ashamed, when he cometh in the glory of his Father with the holy angels. - St. Mark 8:34-38

How to Overcome Your Fear

My brother, my sister, you have to overcome your moral fear. The first step of deliverance is through denying yourself. This means you have to take up your cross and allow yourself to suffer the shame and ridicule that comes with having Christian morals and standards. Think about this, even if you are not a Christian and yet possess characteristics that are morally good, because the world is filled with sin and evil, you will still face opposition. No man has ever set out to do some good, and did not face opposition.

To side with the majority is attempting to save your soul from ridicule and persecution in favor of the majorities praises and recognition. By seeking an alliance through compromise with an evil and adulteress generation is to sacrifice your soul in the snare of fear. What matters most is what happens in the end when you stand before God. Jesus will be ashamed of you before His father and the holy angels. You will have gained the world, but you lose your soul in a lake of fire and brimstone *(Revelation 21:8)*.

The second step of deliverance from moral fear is to believe the gospel. The gospel is the power of God that is able to save your soul. It will keep you from compromising your faith and standards for living. Apostle Paul said this:

> For I am not ashamed of the gospel of Christ: for it is the power of God unto salvation to every one that believeth; to the Jew first, and also to the Greek. - Romans 1:16

The key word here is salvation, which comes from the Greek term "soteria." This means to rescue from harm or to bring one through safely without harm. It is through the gospel of Jesus Christ that you will be able make it through this life without being dominated by sinful pleasures and the temptation to engage in sin..

The third step that I recommend is to pray for boldness. In the book of Acts chapter 4:13-22, Peter and John were threatened by the Jewish council at Jerusalem to not speak any more in the name of Jesus Christ. Instead of compromising the work of God in their lives, to appease the Jewish council, they gathered with their brethren, and prayed for boldness to speak the word of God. Even these disciples who walked with Christ had to pray for courage in order to avoid the snare of fear. How much more should you:

- Deny yourself the praises and recognition of men?
- Believe the gospel for salvation and prosperity?
- Pray for boldness to stand for and speak what is right?

Physical Fear

Physical fear will strip you of your courage that may require physical engagement to do the will of God. It will hamper your ability to respond responsibly in fear of threats of hardships or difficulty in responsibility. Evidence that this type of fear has taken you over is "immobility." You have become intimidated and have lost the motivation to move forward.

In 1 Samuel 17:1-11, Saul and the armies of Israel were intimidated and immobilized because of the size and threat of the Philistine champion, Goliath. The threat of the giant caused Saul and the armies of Israel to see him as being impossible to defeat. This caused them to worry and lose courage. The result of their intimidation caused them not to advance in battle. They were afraid to move forward.

In Numbers 13:32-33, the spies, after viewing the land of milk and honey; returned with a report of the Promised Land and evidence to verify the report as legitimate. However, the report revealed that the children of Anak, giants lived in the land, and the surrounding areas were inhabited by their enemies. Caleb, exercising his faith in the promise of God was ready and willing to go up and take it. However, the spirit of fear engulfed the other spies, leading them to complain. They spoke words of discouragement and became a stumbling block to the faith of Israel.

Note again how this spirit works. It will cause you to look at your situation, engulf you with intimidation, blinding you to the promises of God's deliverance and providence, while filling your mind with excuses, placing you in a mode of immobility and fear.

In Numbers 14:1-4, the spirit of fear swept through the entire congregation, causing them to cry out in complaints against Moses and Aaron. Their next move was to go back to Egypt; a place of minor eases and torments.

If you are not moving forward in God and life, because of hardships, your immobility will soon lead you backwards, leaving you in a position of unfulfilled purpose and destiny. The giants of life can strike you with fear; sapping your courage and strength.

The Causes of Physical Fear

The cause of this fear is intimidation. Webster defines intimidation as being compelled or deterred by or as if by threats. When a person is intimidated, their courage or spirit is broken and beaten down through arrogance, insults, and aggression, they are made to feel inferior and ultimately frightening them into submission. This was the tactic of Goliath.

His arrogance or attitude of superiority came from the many soldiers he had killed in the past. He used his size as a tool of intimidation and his voice to make the armies of Israel feel inferior and ill equipped to fight him. And it worked.

Have you been called to the ministry? You know God said go and preach my word. Spread the gospel. Evangelize. However, a giant named fear has told you that you are not qualified; you do not possess the speech and the look to do the work of God. You may fear you are too young or too old and no one will listen to you.

You have a desire to go back school and finish your degree. You know it will help you to build a better life for your family and/or yourself. However, a voice has told you, that you are too old; it is to too late; you cannot and will not complete it. If you have yielded to these voices, a giant named fear has immobilized you.

You want that promotion and feel like you deserve it. You went to school, you have the skill, and you know you can do the job better than the one who has the position. However, somebody told you that you were not qualified and was not fit for the position. They may have even fired you and told you they were not good enough and they had to replace you.

Maybe you wanted to start a business and the people that you have trusted in, told you that you cannot do it, criticized your goal, and ridiculed you for even thinking up the idea.

Like the spies that saw the land that God promised them; you see the vision plan in your head. You know, if you pursue your dream or do the will of God, your prosperity will increase, your purpose will be fulfilled, and you will reach your God-given destiny. However, you heeded the words of the giant and now the task seems impossible to achieve. As a result, you have become immobile and have given up your dreams. Fear has ensnared you.

How to Overcome Your Fear

First things first, if God has called you to the ministry, to help in ministry, or do a specific task, doing nothing is living in disobedience. When you live in disobedience, you either refuse or fail to obey the command of God. Fear or cowardice is not an excuse.

If you feel like you are too young, to operate in ministry, Paul told Timothy to, "Let no man despise thy youth *(1 Timothy 4:12)"*. He was commanded to go forth and be an example before the believers, in word, life, love, power, faith, and purity. The life that he would live would not be by his own power, nor would he be living unto himself. The people would hear him, and see his example, would follow him, and in the end, be saved.

If you think, you do not have the qualifications or the resources to do the work, consider Moses's call to the ministry. In Exodus chapter 4:1-9, Moses complained stating that the people would not hear him. God gave him a staff and transformed it to a serpent, then back to a staff, afterwards, he was instructed to put his hand on his chest and when he removed it, it was leprous, when he put it back and removed it again, it was normal. God proved to Moses that his power would be working with him to prove to the masses and pharaoh that God was with him.

Moses then complained that he was not a man of eloquent speech *(vs 10-17)*. Fear, even after God revealed to Moses that He would be with him, yet gripped his mind. Moses was holding on to it. God provided Aaron as his spokesperson and told him that he would teach him what to say, and use him to instruct Aaron and he would be his spokesperson.

God removed the excuses for not going forth through the assurance that He would be with him. God qualified him and gave him the resources he needed to do the work.

Secondly, if you have dreams and desires to move forward and beyond where you are in life, you cannot let the voices of the giants of doubt, arrogance, and fear make you feel inferior and unqualified to achieve your goals.

> I can do all things through Christ which strengtheneth me. - Philippians 4:13

Like the power of God to Moses, the power of God through Christ will rest upon you, enabling you to overcome your fears and face your giants.

Face Your Fear

The first step of deliverance from physical fear is to face your fear. "Facing your fear," means to identify or examine the threat that stands before you. Realize that the thing that is holding you back is a spirit working through those who do not want to see you move forward, and/or is making the challenge seem more than what it really is.

Young David heard the words of the Philistine giant, and was actually motivated to accept the challenge. When he stood before Saul, the voice of fear spoke against him, disqualifying him for the task by saying, he was just a youth, and Goliath was a man of war from his youth. Read David's response:

> And David said unto Saul, Thy servant kept his father's sheep, and there came a lion, and a bear, and took a lamb out of the flock: And I went out after him, and smote him, and delivered it out of his mouth: and when he arose against me, I caught him by

his beard, and smote him, and slew him. Thy servant slew both the lion and the bear: and this uncircumcised Philistine shall be as one of them, seeing he hath defied the armies of the living God. David said moreover, The LORD that delivered me out of the paw of the lion, and out of the paw of the bear, he will deliver me out of the hand of this Philistine. And Saul said unto David, Go, and the LORD be with thee. 1 Samuel 17:34-37

David's testimony was how the power of God prevailed in his life, through the previous trials he'd experienced. The voice of fear will cause you to forget the miracles that the Lord had previously worked in your life. You have to remember where God has brought you from. Doing this will allow you to see the enemy of fear for what it really is, a threat, and nothing more. Remember when you face down your giant, it will magnify itself the more. When David approached Goliath, He belittled him again, but David was not deterred; he trusted in his God.

The second step in facing your fear is that after you have identified it, let your fear know that you see it for what it really is, state your position in God, and speak victory in advance. Read David's words:

Then said David to the Philistine, Thou comest to me with a sword, and with a spear, and with a shield: but I come to thee in the name of the LORD of hosts, the God of the armies of Israel, whom thou hast defied. This day will the LORD deliver thee into mine hand; and I will smite thee, and take thine head from thee; and I will give the carcases of the host of the Philistines this day unto the fowls of the air, and to the wild beasts of the earth; that all the earth may know that there is a God in Israel. And all this assembly shall know that the LORD saveth not with sword and spear: for the battle is the LORD's, and he will give you into our hands. 1 Samuel 17:45 - 47

The Third step is to engage. Do the work and charge forward in the power of God. Do not prepare to defeat just one giant; there will be others to fight, these are the trials that come afterwards.

David chose five smooth stones. One for Goliath and four more for his four brothers, he did not intend to miss, but was ready to be persistent in battle.

Realize who you are in Christ and the power he has invested in you. Go forward and break out of the snare of fear.

Spiritual Fear

Spiritual fears hinder your spiritual and emotional well-being. Usually, these types of fears come from your past hurts, imaginations, or demonic engagements such as night terrors. These types of fears cause anxieties, phobias, and depression. Let's look at these three elements to get a better understanding of what encompass spiritual fears.

Anxiety

Anxiety describes an inner turmoil that is manifested through nervous behavior like trembling, pacing, sweating, jitters, and irrational talk. Anxiety "subjects its victims to fear by causing an overreaction" to a situation or object that is perceived as a threat.

Anxiety is a higher form of worry. When extreme anxiety becomes apparent, the tormented soul is thrown into a repetitive cycle of defense, doing whatever they can to avoid the perceived event that would bring them harm. Some people lose control and suffer panic attacks or palpitations, which are rapid and irregular heartbeats. These attacks come about abruptly and last from minutes to hours; they can even cause violent reactions.

Phobias

Anxieties are symptoms of "phobias." Phobias are fears intensified over things that could be real, but pose little to no danger at all. In some cases, the phobia is imagined, an intense and unreal fear formed from a traumatic event.

Phobias can encompass virtually anything from insects to elevators, closed places to public places. Some people fear going outside, so they lock themselves indoors in order to avoid people or places that are synonymous with the traumatic event. Some people fear sickness and disease and find themselves constantly cleaning as to avoid germs. Some people become anti-social, distrusting, and refusing to talk to anyone or enter into new relationships because of a horrible breakup, divorce, or bad relationship. Other types of Phobias are:

- **Fear of being alone**: This fear comes from a bad divorce in which you were rejected or death of a loved one.
- **Fear of darkness:** This fear comes from not being able to see if something is in the room or fearing that something is in the room with you. It can relate to being locked in closed places, imagining seeing figures in the dark and hearing things.
- **Fear of failure:** Overworking to avoid failure, feel like your work won't be accepted. You feel you're not smart enough. You entertain obsessive thoughts about your work.
- **Fear of intimacy:** You won't entertain new relationships because you fear being hurt. Avoid sexual contact with your spouse because of past abuse or hurts.
- **Fear of demons:** This fear comes from having night terrors. You sleep with the light on; you find it hard to sleep because of intrusive thoughts of previous attacks.

Night Terrors

There have been many cases where people, having gone to sleep and felt a presence sitting on their chest, smuggling their ability to talk and move. Usually this event is accompanied with a nightmare that's associated with a horrible dream of being chased, falling, or running. Some have awakened from these dreams and seeing the dark shadowy figure that caused the haunting. These are real demons attempting to strike your heart with fear.

My Personal Experience

I have had my own personal experiences with this spirit. One night I laid down to sleep and found myself, not too long after falling asleep, paralyzed. I could not move. I could feel a tightening around my legs. Somehow, I was able to see a large white snake wrapped around my legs, but I could not see the head. I struggled to scream out, "JESUS." The more I said his name; it would loosen its grip.

Finally, when I was free, I woke up and could still feel the tightening loosen. Now, this had to be spiritual, because in my mind, the moment, I woke up. I saw it slither down the steps. I got up and anointed my entire home that night.

However, something else happened. I began to worry if that spirit would come back, whenever I would lay down to sleep. I found myself sleeping with the bathroom light on and taking a little longer to fall asleep. Because of this, I believe I allowed that spirit to come back and attack again. However, this time the attacks were different. I could always tell when it was going to happen because when I could feel myself going to sleep, I could feel something on my bed move, as if someone sat on it. Finally, after suffering so many attacks, I was fed-up. I went on a fast and prayed over my home. This time turned out all the lights and declared peace in my home. I refused to feed thoughts to those incidents again. Like I previously stated, Fear starts and ends in the mind.

Where Does It Start?

I have to admit that, I was a fan of horror movies. I loved watching certain channels on television that highlighted all horror movies and I was a fan. I noticed also that my daughter has been always afraid of going to bed at night. In the middle of the night, she would always wake her mother and bring her into her room to sleep with her. This happened up until she was the age of 11.

Therefore, I decided to not watch horror movies anymore, nor look at what I considered my favorite channel. I prayed and anointed my home and the night terrors stopped. I honestly believe that some horror movies are doorways for evil spirits to travel through and enter the home, especially those that deal with demon possession and witchcraft.

Horror movies are designed to strike fear into the mind. This is where fear starts. Another definition for fear is "Phobos" from which we get the English word "phobia," meaning, "dread" or "terror" resulting from a thought, seeded from a traumatizing experience. This type of spirit is demonic in nature, connecting with the roots of issues or events found in a person's history, current or previous indulgences, or experiences.

- Abuse, Child Abuse, Church Abuse, Sexual Abuse
- Loss of a loved one, friend
- Witness a death or having a near death experience

- Relationship (Divorce, Constant Breakups, Bad Social Influences)
- Sickness (fear of germs, disease)
- Horror shows or anything designed to strike intense fear

Depression

Phobias cause Depression, which is extreme sadness or melancholy *(feeling low in spirit)*. Depression can result in slothfulness in business and life engagement. This is where the spirit of fear, after its torments, begins its binding of the soul. The depressed begin to make excuses for their depression, believing that there is no end to their dark struggle.

Victims of depression describe it as "living in a black hole." The black hole experience is feeling hopeless, lifeless, and empty. The depressed can fall into slothfulness, not having any energy or motivation to pursue and enjoy life. Then there is the feeling of impending doom, which is always having the feeling that something bad is going to happen. This feeling is the demon itself, snaring the soul into depression.

The enemy spirit pushes negative, intrusive thoughts into your mind, interrupting your normal mode of thinking and ability to function. This causes irritability, anger, frustration, low self-esteem, excessive crying and in some cases, reckless behavior. Once fear has totally gripped your mind and has taken control of your emotions, it will cause you to entertain suicidal thoughts and tendencies. The voice of this demon will plant thoughts in your mind, making you think and say words like:

- Maybe I should just kill myself.
- I feel trapped and I need to get out.
- The world or people will be better off without me.

Fear is an oppressive and tormenting spirit that exercises unlawful authority and power over your mind body and life. You have to break free in order to live and love again. Jesus ministry was all about healing those that suffered oppression by the devil *(Acts 10:38)*.

How to Overcome Your Fear

> There is no fear in love; but perfect love casteth out fear: because fear hath torment. He that feareth is not made perfect in love. - 1 John 4:18

The key to breaking this spirit is to realize how much God loves you, and allow His love to be perfected in you. Is your phobia "loneliness"? Do you fear that you may be alone for the rest of your life and that no one will ever love you? Maybe, someone you loved dearly died and now you feel like that love could never be replaced? Maybe you fear intimacy due to a bad break-up and/or suffered a horrible relationship. Do you feel like a failure? Are you constantly worried about being accepted? Do you feel low, unqualified, or not good enough? Do you fear the dark and the unknown, suffering night terrors and abandonment by God?

In all of these situations, the enemy has blinded you to the fact of one of the Lord's greatest promises:

> lo, I am with you always, even unto the end of the world. Amen.
> - St. Matthew 28:20b

No matter the condition of your soul and spirit, the Lord Jesus Christ has promised to be with you always. He has taken notice of every detail within your struggles and your sufferings; he knows the causes and the roots of evil that has settled in your mind and has a plan to bring you deliverance. Read the words of our Lord:

> If ye shall ask any thing in my name, I will do it. If ye love me, keep my commandments. And I will pray the Father, and he shall give you another Comforter, that he may abide with you for ever; Even the Spirit of truth; whom the world cannot receive, because it seeth him not, neither knoweth him: but ye know him; for he dwelleth with you, and shall be in you. I will not leave you comfortless: I will come to you. Yet a little while, and the world seeth me no more; but ye see me: because I live, ye shall live also. At that day ye shall know that I am in my Father, and ye in me, and I in you. He that hath my commandments, and keepeth them, he it is that loveth me: and he that loveth me shall be loved

of my Father, and I will love him, and will manifest myself to him. - St. John 14:14-21

In order to experience Gods love through Jesus Christ, you have to accept him as Lord and Savior, ask him to come into your heart, and he will abide with you forever. The spirit of fear will then be flushed from your soul and mind. God will then fill you with his presence and power, taking over thoughts and filling your mind with the things that are lovely, true, and honest and of good report.

> Be careful for nothing; but in everything by prayer and supplication with thanksgiving let your requests be made known unto God. And the peace of God, which passeth all understanding, shall keep your hearts and minds through Christ Jesus. Finally, brethren, whatsoever things are true, whatsoever things are honest, whatsoever things are just, whatsoever things are pure, whatsoever things are lovely, whatsoever things are of good report; if there be any virtue, and if there be any praise, think on these things.- Philippians 4:6-8

Heed the instruction of the scripture: Think on the things that are:

- **True:** Speak the truth, live the truth in recognizing and allowing the word of God to guide your life. Meditate on his word daily. *(Psalms 1:1-3)*
- **Honest:** Mediating on the word will rid your mind of any preconceived ideas that blinded your mind from the truth of God's word. Think no evil. Think positively, according to the word, even when it comes to the people around you. *(2 Corinthians 8:21)*
- **Just:** Be an example of righteousness and holiness. Treat people fairly and expect the same for yourself. Do the right thing, never compromise. *(Deuteronomy 16:20)*
- **Pure:** Be careful of what you watch and what you hear. Your mind is a recorder. Guard your spirit from the very appearance of evil. *(1 Thessalonians 1:22)*
- **Lovely:** follow charity, do not be envious of others and their fortune, do not be rash, irritated, or angry at anothers fortune, but be happy for them. Rejoice in the truth and

hope for a better end for yourself and others. *(1 Corinthians 13:4-7)*

Build your character on moral excellence according to the word of God and He will establish your well-being and happiness. This peace of God will engulf your mind building your boldness and courage to face your fears.

Courage

Your spiritual courage is built through prayer and controlling your thoughts through the word of God. Worry and anxiety are overcome through persistent prayer. God will renew your focus on his promises and strengthen your confidence in his power.

As your mind begins to restore, take note of how your courage will begin to unfold in these three areas: You will experience:

- **Physical Courage:** Which is being able to engage your hardships and difficulties in pursuing your purpose, destiny, and the will of God for your life.
- **Spiritual Courage:** Which is grabbing a hold of your mind, emotions, and rebuking the powers of darkness that haunt, allowing you to face your fears in the power of God.
- **Moral Courage:** Which is standing up for your Christian standards without compromise, even in the face of ridicule and persecution.

Remember the fowler is a liar; the images and thoughts that he uses to trigger panic in the mind are not true and do not bear the danger projected. Your courage will come from your confidence in the provision and promises of God.

Overcoming the spirit of fear is about changing your perception of life by looking through the word of God and letting his spirit and power dwell in you. Allow the change to happen. Allow the negative imprints on your mind to be erased, and visualize your future as bright and prosperous. Before you realize it, you will be walking free from the snare and in the joy of the Lord

Chapter Ten

The Lustful Spirit

The Lustful Spirit

Men are naturally attracted to women and women are naturally attracted to men. If a man sees a nude woman or a woman sees a nude man, if they are suitable too the eyes and appeal to the desire of the looker, it is only a natural response to feel aroused. As human beings, we cannot expect to remain unstimulated when exposed to the nudity of the opposite sex. That is the way the God designed it. Sex is not an evil act, when it is between two married people and within the context of holiness. Satan corrupts and perverts this natural attraction through lust.

Lust is one of the most devious and snaring demons in the kingdom of Satan. It is an extreme corruption of human desire. The influence of lust is so devious; it breeds an uncontrollable habit of longing for sexual fulfillment, while nullifying your ability to gain self-control. Where there is no self-control, lust causes addiction. It has the power to override all other desires. It becomes an intense and unrestrained sexual craving that overwhelms the thoughts and traps the spirit of a person in many types of sexual and unwholesome acts of debauchery.

The second reason why lust is so devious is that lust itself is not an outside force. Lust comes from within. It comes from our own inward desires and inclinations.

> Let no man say when he is tempted, I am tempted of God: for
> God cannot be tempted with evil, neither tempteth he any man:
> But every man is tempted, when he is drawn away of his own
> lust, and enticed. Then when lust hath conceived, it bringeth forth
> sin: and sin, when it is finished, bringeth forth death. Do not err,
> my beloved brethren. - James 1:13 16

In the story of David and Bathsheba, David was drawn away from the will of God by his own lust in fulfilling the act of adultery with Bathsheba. After she notified him that she was pregnant, He went from one extreme to the next. David sought to cover up his sin and in failing to do so; he murdered Uriah, Bathsheba's husband. This act of lust brought about turmoil and death to the house of David.

In 2 Samuel 13:1-32, we find that David's son, Amnon is vexed with a lustful spirit, desiring his own sister, Tamar, who was a virgin. When lust conceived in his heart, he sought out to satisfy his lust through subtle means; resulting in her rape. After the act was committed, guilt set in and he went from one extreme to the next. His lust, after the act was committed moved him to hate. Like his father, he sought to cover his actions by telling her to keep silent. However, Absalom, Tamar and Amnon's brother found out about the act. When the opportunity for vengeance came, he avenged Tamar by having Amnon killed.

In each case, both parties sought to cover up their sin, which only led to another act of sin, which soon led to exposure and death. Lust is insidious. Once this spirit has snared your soul, there is no telling what immoral acts it may lead you to commit.

> For out of the heart proceed evil thought, murders, adulteries,
> fornications, thefts, false witness, blasphemies, - St. Matthew
> 15:19

God never sends tests of faith that are associated with sin, neither does he tempt or try you with sin. Remember, because of your former relationship with Satan, he knows what makes you tick.

Seven Steps In Temptation

If you study Eve's temptation in the Garden of Eden, you will notice seven steps that Satan used to deter her into temptation:

- **He starts with a thought. Genesis 3:4** - And the serpent said unto the woman, Ye shall not surely die: For God doth know that in the day ye eat thereof, then your eyes shall be opened, and ye shall be as gods, knowing good and evil. He removed the consequence of her actions and inserted a pleasurable idea. Once you entertain the idea in your mind, you are then-

- **Drawn away or pulled away from God's will with a strong imagination.** Genesis 3:6, Eve desired to be wise like God. She wanted to enjoy the feeling of being like God. Concerning lust, you want to feel good, relaxed and enjoy the pleasure that the act brings.

- **The Tool of sin looks good.** It's attractive. The thing desired looks good to the eyes. The tree was pleasant to look at and the fruit was good for indulgence (Genesis 3:6). Lust in whatever form it's presented to you, looks good. The person or image you're looking at appeals to your joy.

- **Lust or the desire to commit the act is planted in the heart.** The will to resist has been overcome. Your flesh is then aroused and now, you want it

- **Lust has now taken root.** Eve takes the fruit. She yields to the temptation. You have entertained the thought and now you scheme and find ways to make it happen.

- **Sin is committed.** She eats the fruit. She indulges and gives to her husband. You indulge in the act.

- **Death occurs.** The eyes of Adam and Eve were opened, and they realized that they were naked and were ashamed. You recognized that what you have done was wrong and guilt set in to prove this. However, just as Adam and Eve hid themselves from God, sin has separated you from Him.

What you did not realize was that once you have broken the hedge of protection around you by yielding to the temptation of sexual lust, you allowed the enemy to affect your thoughts with the things that your flesh desires. The bite of the serpent yields a poison that imprints the images of the very thing that led to the temptation in your mind. These images will appear at the most inconvenient times, drawing you into the same seven steps, repeatedly.

The Snares of Lust

> Now the works of the flesh are manifest, which are these;
> Adultery, fornication, uncleanness, lasciviousness, - Galatians
> 5:19

The first four fleshly works are sexual in nature. These are
branches of lust at work. And they have a snaring effect.

Adultery

Adultery or "moichos" is sexual relations between a married
person and a single individual. Adultery is a high level of coveting,
defined as "desiring something that belongs to someone else."
Adultery in these current times is more prevalent than it was years
ago. Satan has upped the ante, and has baited many "so-called"
unfulfilled Christians into various types of sexual sins that can and
has destroyed their walk with God, marriages and social
relationships. Consider the words of our Lord:

> Ye have heard that it was said by them of old time, Thou shalt
> not commit adultery: But I say unto you, That whosoever looketh
> on a woman to lust after her hath committed adultery with her
> already in his heart.- Matthew 5:27-28

The spirit of adultery is a spirit that works against troubled
marriages and marriage in general. It violates and breaks the bond of
the marriage. Satan analyzes the issues that couples struggle with,
and uses those struggles as a means to snare one or both spouses into
acts of adultery.

The intriguing thing about adultery is that the spouse has to be
willing to engage in the act. They have to make a conscience choice
to do so. Bathsheba was very much at fault in the act while David
operated deceitfully to cover up his actions.

In the Old Testament, adultery is so vile, that if either spouse
were caught in the act, death by stoning was warranted.

> If a damsel that is a virgin be betrothed unto a husband, and a
> man find her in the city, and lie with her; Then ye shall bring
> them both out unto the gate of that city, and ye shall stone them

with stones that they die; the damsel, because she cried not, being in the city; and the man, because he hath humbled his neighbor's wife: so thou shalt put away evil from among you. - Deuteronomy 22:23-24

Online Adultery

There are those who believe that adultery on the internet is not possible. However, what they fail to understand is that the internet is a society within itself. Social media is a construct of sites where people can engage in conversations using chat software, phone, and visual software. Satan has taken advantage of these tools as baits to snare wandering eyes into lust. Spouses are now engaging secretly via internet in acts of adultery. Remember the words of our Lord:

> Ye have heard that it was said by them of old time, Thou shalt not commit adultery: But I say unto you, That whosoever looketh on a woman to lust after her hath committed adultery with her already in his heart.- Matthew 5:27-28

Consenting Adultery

In the Book of Galatians Chapter 5:21, the scripture mentions the term "revellings." In the Greek, revellings come from the word "orgy" meaning sex party. Sex parties involve groups or like-minded couples, coming together and freely engage in open and unrestrained sexual activity.

Open relationships or swinging couples claim to love each other above anything and anyone. However, because there is a lack of sexual satisfaction, they seek out other partners to satisfy their sexual need. They believe that the process avoids the idea of cheating, betrayal, and heartache. No matter the reason for having such a relationship, it is a violation of the law of God and is the workings of a lustful spirit.

Emotional Adultery

Adultery or having an affair can begin innocently. Two people who have common interests can become friends. They spend time together in conversation, in-person, via chat or phone and can become emotionally attached. Even though both individuals may never come together, each has feelings for one another. The man can become protective and caring for the other woman and the woman can become dependent on the care of the man. Both begin to share feelings or secrets that should only be known to the spouse. This is emotional adultery. Soon these emotions begin to separate both parties from their spouses.

This type of adultery attacks the foundation of a marriage indirectly. It slowly eats away the foundation of a couple's love, causing emotional distances and lack of concern within the marriage. At this point, all it takes is one encounter where the parties are left alone. This is just one way the spirit of lust can destroy a marriage through a false sense of love.

Being married requires you to be careful of whom you befriend, and talk too often. Emotional adultery can start within marriage that lacks communication. One spouse's feelings can be easily enticed through conversation and attention from an outsider.

Be careful of statements that say, "We're just friends, nothing more." If your spouse has to ask you why you and your new friend are spending so much time together, maybe you should call the friendship off. Other signs of emotional adultery are in conversations where the friend is always mentioned, when it's not warranted. The spirit of lust is slowly drawing you away. It has used your desire for communication and attention to draw you away, slowly into the trap of adultery.

The Consequences of Adultery

You have read about David's reaping because of his act of lust. Adultery yields consequences that bring judgments against one's own soul. Adultery violates the bond of trust and voids precious memories of marital events gained down through the years. Adultery robs the spouse of peace, self-esteem and destroys the foundation of the family. Adultery can lead to bitterness and unforgiveness. Heed the words of Solomon, concerning adultery.

> To keep thee from the evil woman, from the flattery of the tongue of a strange woman. Lust not after her beauty in thine heart; neither let her take thee with her eyelids. For by means of a whorish woman a man is brought to a piece of bread: and the

adultress will hunt for the precious life. Can a man take fire in his bosom, and his clothes not be burned? Can one go upon hot coals, and his feet not be burned? So he that goeth in to his neighbour's wife; whosoever toucheth her shall not be innocent. Men do not despise a thief, if he steal to satisfy his soul when he is hungry; But if he be found, he shall restore sevenfold; he shall give all the substance of his house. But whoso committeth adultery with a woman lacketh understanding: he that doeth it destroyeth his own soul. A wound and dishonour shall he get; and his reproach shall not be wiped away. For jealousy is the rage of a man: therefore he will not spare in the day of vengeance. He will not regard any ransom; neither will he rest content, though thou givest many gifts. - Proverbs 6:24-35

A man or woman violated by an outsider cannot be won over by gifts of apology, for tearing down a home and family through adultery. The husband or wife can become so bitter behind the act, that they could become vindictive and pursue harmful means to both parties involved. The hurting soul can become driven by a jealous rage.

Fornication

Fornication is sexual relations between two people who are not married. Society has been deceived into believing that sex outside of marriage is just an event of pleasure and signs of affection, between a man and woman. Fornication is actually a form of idolatry. In Latin terms, fornication comes from "fornix" which means "brothel." A brothel was a place where harlots or prostitutes could be purchased for sexual favors. Another type of harlot offered herself as a sexual tool in religious worship to a false god in biblical times.

Idolatry in its most simplistic definition is the worship of idols. This worship involved a blind admiration, adoration, or devotion to a person or thing. It does not have to be a deity. In false god worship in biblical times, engaging in acts of fornication before idol gods was a worship norm in society, but abominable in the sight of God.

This act extends into pornographic films, pictures and books *(Ephesians 5:3)*. Another Greek term for fornication comes from "Porneia" which encompasses many terms such as incest, adultery, and pornography or "Porneis" which is illicit sexual intercourse.

Engaging in pornography or fornication is a sin against one's own soul, because it creates spiritual ties through evil imaginations and spirits, either via internet or via person. The soul tie is "a spiritual and mental link or cleaving that holds two or more people together." In Rome, the people forsook the ordinances of God and made themselves gods, and through acts of fornication, they worshipped those gods. This is idolatry.

> Because that which may be known of God is manifest in them; for God hath shewed it unto them. For the invisible things of him from the creation of the world are clearly seen, being understood by the things that are made, even his eternal power and Godhead; so that they are without excuse: Because that, when they knew God, they glorified him not as God, neither were thankful; but became vain in their imaginations, and their foolish heart was darkened. Professing themselves to be wise, they became fools, And changed the glory of the uncorruptible God into an image made like to corruptible man, and to birds, and fourfooted beasts, and creeping things. Wherefore God also gave them up to uncleanness through the lusts of their own hearts, to dishonour their own bodies between themselves: Who changed the truth of God into a lie, and worshipped and served the creature more than the Creator, who is blessed for ever. Amen. - Romans 1:19-25

Pornography and Masturbation

Engaging in pornography ties one's soul to the demons of lust through the act of masturbation.

> What? Know ye not that he which is joined to an harlot is one body? for two, saith he, shall be one flesh. But he that is joined unto the Lord is one spirit. Flee fornication. Every sin that a man doeth is without the body; but he that committeth fornication sinneth against his own body. - 1 Corinthians 6:16:18

This is why it is so hard for a person to break from the binding cords of lust. To engage in fornication and masturbation is willingly giving your soul over to demonic spirits. The same goes if you give yourself over to someone who has a disturbed spirit, you give yourself over to be tied with the same spirit they have. The demonic spirit can become your master and fill your spirit and mind with the desire to engage more and more, constantly driving you into acts that never satisfy the desire.

Pornography and masturbation destroy the home and marriage. Men and women bound by this spirit have entered relationships, believing that if they are married, they will have access to sex whenever they want it, and curb their lust, just to find out that the woman or man they married could not satisfy their lust. They remain accustomed to the porn stimulus and the act of masturbation. This is one way marriages are destroyed.

Pornography soon replaces the spouse. The spouse can never reach a point of satisfaction because the models on the internet have become the only means of stimulation. In this case, men who engage in masturbation and porn often, suffer from erectile dysfunction, when engaging in sex with their spouse. Pornography has become the only means of fantasy for the man and can never be matched by the spouse.

Masturbation reduces a person's need for intimacy and when out of control, ruins a person's social life. Images and thoughts about porn constantly intrude and occupy the mind, driving one to perform the act. The constant indulgence drains motivation and energy to do business. Soon procrastination sets in and responsibilities are neglected.

Dopamine

Pornography when mixed with masturbation releases a chemical in the brain called "dopamine." Dopamine is a neurochemical that helps control the brain's pleasure centers, assists with regulation of movement, control of emotions, causes you to recognize the benefits and rewards in opportunities, and assists with the motivation to pursue them.

Porn floods the brain with dopamine, causing cells within the brain to shut down receptors. When the receptors are reduced, a lesser amount of dopamine floods the brain. The result is less energy, depression, and guilt. Soon life itself becomes less exciting. However, the pleasure centers of the brain need dopamine in order to make you feel happy, so you are drawn even more to pornography as a stimulus and the cycle continues over and over and over.

Therefore, the drive to seek out more porn is shifted into hyper-drive.

As this desire increases, the stimulus becomes less effective. This is the dangerous part, because now the intensity required to be satisfied, will have to increase. It will require a more intense pleasure, which leads the snared to seek out other acts that are even more low and evil to satisfy the craving.

Dopamine is not wrong. Your brain produces it. Satan and his demons use it against you by driving your desires with pornography. Dopamine creates an intense desire for sex. The more it is released into the brain, the desire to be satisfied increases. You literally become addicted to yourself.

Masturbation is highly addictive due to some of the minor benefits it offers. If the spouse is out of town, or one is not married it offers a temporary relief from sexual urges and associated frustrations. However, because of this quick release system, men and women can become mastered by it, not knowing its biological effects. It causes frequent urges that strip you of your ability to maintain self-control.

Masturbation desensitizes a person's affection to the opposite sex, creating only a desire to be sexually fulfilled. The danger that awaits is that it may not matter whom or "what" fulfills that desire. Whatever feels good; you would just go with it. Masturbation does not decrease sexual tension. It only enhances it.

Uncleanness

> Wherefore God also gave them up to uncleanness through the lusts of their own hearts, to dishonour their own bodies between themselves: Who changed the truth of God into a lie, and worshipped and served the creature more than the Creator, who is blessed for ever. Amen. For this cause God gave them up unto vile affections: for even their women did change the natural use into that which is against nature: And likewise also the men, leaving the natural use of the woman, burned in their lust one toward another; men with men working that which is unseemly, and receiving in themselves that recompence of their error which was meet. Romans 1:24-27

Uncleanness is the evil deeds and vices associated with sexual sins. *(Colossians 3:5-Sex toys, pornographic magazines, videos,)* Uncleanness is "akatharsia" which means physical sensuality. Paul addressed this issue to the Roman church, stating that because the people rejected God, he gave them over to dishonour their bodies between themselves, because of their constant indulgences of "loving themselves"; worshiping the creature which was their own bodies.

Such actions committed involve:

- Men with men *(Homosexuality)*
- Women with women *(Lesbianism)*
- Men and women with beasts *(Bestiality)*
- Adults with children *(Pedophilia)*
- Sexual toys

Lasciviousness

Lasciviousness is sexual acts that are void of any moral decency. This involves people performing acts of sex in public. *(2 Corinthians 12:21)* Lasciviousness is "asegeia" or "licentiousness" which means being lawless, rude and disrespectful in a sexual manner. The spirit of lust can drive a person to seek out sexual pleasures in places like porn and video shops, meeting people online and connecting with them in parks for a sexual rendezvous.

These people can connect with each other on the internet and do sexual things that the spouse would not or could not do. These meeting places are inconspicuous and in some cases, public.

Breaking the Lustful Spirit

The first step towards deliverance from masturbation and lust is simple. Turn off the computer, the tablet, or television. Whatever provides you the access, you need to get rid of it.

Second, if you are married and are sexually unfulfilled, you must come together, discuss the issue, and find ways within the context of righteousness to satisfy one another. I say within the context of righteousness, because some spouses have used the vices of uncleanness *(sex toys, porn)* as a means of adding a spark to their sex life, just to find out later that they have been replaced.

Breaking free from masturbation may not be very easy without the help of your spouse. You have to get used to a real person again. One key that I recommend is to not just engage in sex, plan your rendezvous, and romance each other up until the event.

> Let thy fountain be blessed: and rejoice with the wife of thy youth. Let her be as the loving hind and pleasant roe; let her breasts satisfy thee at all times; and be thou ravished always with her love. - Proverbs 5:18-19

For singles, a greater commitment to consecration is needed to overcome this spirit. You will have to submit your body to God through fasting, prayer, and studying Gods word. Fasting crucifies and diminishes the desires of the flesh, prayer gives you strength to resist, and the spirit of God becomes your guide and purges your conscience. However, remember you will have to get rid of the avenues of temptation. Turn it off.

> For this is the will of God, even your sanctification, that ye should abstain from fornication: That every one of you should know how to possess his vessel in sanctification and honour; Not in the lust of concupiscence, even as the Gentiles which know not God: - 1 Thessalonians 4:3-5

You have to sanctify yourself.

Lust and Marriage

> Defraud ye not one the other, except it be with consent for a time, that ye may give yourselves to fasting and prayer; and come together again, that Satan tempt you not for your incontinency.- 1 Corinthians 7:5

In order to avoid lust in marriage, couples must come together in order to avoid this temptation. Doing so helps to maintain self-control and assists in fleshy sufferings during consecration.

Purge Your Mind

> Wherewithal shall a young man cleanse his way? by taking heed thereto according to thy word. With my whole heart have I sought thee: O let me not wander from thy commandments. Thy

word have I hid in mine heart, that I might not sin against thee.- Psalms 119:9-16

After turning off your digital devices, the process of deliverance does not stop there. The next step is to cleanse your mind, by purging out those thoughts and images. This is done by obeying the word of God.

You must give yourself to studying and meditating on the word of God. The word will cleanse you of the thoughts and reasoning's of excuses for falling back into sin.

Sanctify them through thy truth: thy word is truth. - St. John 17:17

Sanctification is the key, because it sets you apart for his usage. This does not mean that the temptations will stop. Your body is used to being satisfied in that manner, and that lustful spirit will surely fire off darts to your mind. Even after, you have overcome it. The temptations will continue, but as you yield yourself over to God, through obedience to the word and much praying and fasting, you will find the draw less and less effective. Deliverance will be yours. You can and you will overcome this. Just do not yield. You have to endure.

Chapter Eleven

The Bitter Spirit

The Spirit of Bitterness

> Follow peace with all men, and holiness, without which no man shall see the Lord: Looking diligently lest any man fail of the grace of God; lest any root of bitterness springing up trouble you, and thereby many be defiled;- Hebrews 12:14-15

"Bitterness" comes from "pikria" which is extreme wickedness or hatred arising from anger because of being mistreated or imagined mistreatment. When a person is offended, they experience extreme annoyance or resentment because of an insult, disregard, or criticism. In order to get to the center of why and how a person becomes bitter, we have to understand the seed from which the root grows.

Understanding the Tree Root System

Roots operate as the conduits of minerals, oxygen, and water from the soil into the tree. During the tree's growth period, roots may store these nutrients during the winter seasons and release them in the springtime for branch, leaf, and trunk development.

The feeder roots grow around the top of the soil where oxygen, water, and minerals are in abundance. If the depth of the topsoil is increased, the weight and covering of the new soil can reduce the amount of oxygen and water intake available to the roots.

Damage can also occur through overwatering. Which also restricts the mineral intake; again causing roots to compete for mineral resources. This results in improper development. If the roots are not handled and cleaned properly, the tree could wither and die. Therefore, the life of the tree rests in the roots.

Application

According Isaiah 61:3, when the Lord saved you and filled you with his spirit, he removed the spirit of heaviness and gave you a garment of praise, making you a tree of righteousness; established firm in the word, giving God glory, honor, and praise.

According to Proverbs 11:30; the fruit of the righteous brings life. This means that after you received the power of the Holy Ghost, you were equipped to win souls for the Lord.

> But ye shall receive power, after that the Holy Ghost is come upon you: and ye shall be witnesses unto me both in Jerusalem, and in all Judæa, and in Samaria, and unto the uttermost part of the earth.-Acts 1:8

The power of the Holy Ghost will give you influence to win souls for Christ. It empowers you to preach the gospel effectively and making the presence of God more real to the hearer. The hearer will not only hear, but will be able to see the power of the gospel working in your life. It's all about influence. That influence is manifested through the fruit of the spirit, which has many seeds:

> But the fruit of the Spirit is love, joy, peace, longsuffering, gentleness, goodness, faith, meekness, temperance: against such there is no law-Galatians 5:22-24

These are manifested through the believer's life, and planted into the heart, that is the root system of the hearer: However, if the believer is offended, then his feeder root system will deliver bitter seed to the heart of the hearer, corrupting his faith and defiling his spirit. It is all about influence *(lest any root of bitterness springing up trouble you, and thereby many be defiled)*.

The Seed of Offense

Bitterness grows from the seed of "offense." The offense itself is a trap. It comes from the Greek term "Skandalon" which is the name of or part of a trap in which a bait is attached. Skandalon or offense refers to anything that transgresses the law of an individual; resulting in hatred or prejudice. Offense itself is not evil. Offense transgresses the law of sin in the lives of the disobedient. Example: According to 1 Peter 2:7-8, Jesus became a stone of stumbling, and a rock of offence to them who were disobedient or refused to adhere to his word.

> And he called the multitude, and said unto them, Hear, and understand: Not that which goeth into the mouth defileth a man; but that which cometh out of the mouth, this defileth a man. Then came his disciples, and said unto him, Knowest thou that the Pharisees were offended, after they heard this saying? But he answered and said, Every plant, which my heavenly Father hath not planted, shall be rooted up. Let them alone: they be blind leaders of the blind. And if the blind lead the blind, both shall fall into the ditch.-St. Matthew 15:11-14

The Pharisees found the words of Jesus offensive because he transgressed their tradition and proved them as hypocrites, in the eyes of God and before the people. He questioned their rule by saying, "why do ye transgress the commandment of God by your tradition?" And called them out publically, correcting them of their sin. To add insult to injury, he called forth the multitudes and taught a word that was the complete opposite of what they believed and taught. Peter revealed to Jesus that the Pharisees were offended at his word. He responded by telling them that their offense was a result of not being true to the word of God, nor were they true followers.

The Pharisees were not the only ones offended by the word of Jesus. When Jesus taught in the synagogue in his own hometown, his people were offended by his words.

> And it came to pass, that when Jesus had finished these parables, he departed thence. And when he was come into his own country, he taught them in their synagogue, insomuch that they were astonished, and said, Whence hath this man this wisdom, and these mighty works? Is not this the carpenter's son? is not his mother called Mary? and his brethren, James, and Joses, and Simon, and Judas? And his sisters, are they not all with us? Whence then hath this man all these things? And they were

offended in him. But Jesus said unto them, A prophet is not without honour, save in his own country, and in his own house. And he did not many mighty works there because of their unbelief. - St. Matthew 13:53-58

In each case, the snare of offense was revealed. The people in Nazareth were corrected by the wisdom of words spoken by Jesus Christ. The seed of offense caused them to see him only as the son of Joseph and Mary, and as a mere carpenter, not a messiah.

In addition, the seed offense caused a rise of unbelief among the people, which soon led to their rejection of Jesus Christ, hindering the power of God operating in that place. Offense blinded them, to the truth of the gospel, leaving them in darkness and not being able to see the error of their ways.

He that is first in his own cause seemeth just; but his neighbour cometh and searcheth him. The lot causeth contentions to cease, and parteth between the mighty. A brother offended is harder to be won than a strong city: and their contentions are like the bars of a castle. A man's belly shall be satisfied with the fruit of his mouth; and with the increase of his lips shall he be filled. Proverbs 18:19

Every person's lives their life by a code, which has been deemed good or necessary for their living. However, when a person; as Jesus did here, comes along and violates that code by challenging it and counting it as an incorrect, bad and an unnecessary way of life, the listener can become offended; which can lead to blinding them to what may be the truth.

Instead of accepting correction, Satan magnifies the feelings of offense by making you feel affronted, disregarded or made low, sending you into a tirade of emotions that will ultimately lead to the watering of the offensive seed; sprouting forth roots of bitterness, which then grows; making you a tree of unrighteousness.

When Satan traps you in offense, it is hard to pursue peace with you, and for you to follow peace with the offender.

Esau and the Birthright

Some offenses come because of disregard for holy things and personal failures. Whenever holy things are disregarded as nothing, personal failure before God becomes evident and the price paid can be catastrophic.

Esau sold his birthright for a momentary, mere satisfaction of the flesh. The blessing and birthrights consisted of rights, responsibilities, and honors associated with being the firstborn. However, Esau forfeited those rights by selling his birthright to Jacob for a pot of lentils and bread. This was how much value he placed on receiving his birthright and the blessings of God.

> Now Jacob deceived his father into blessing him with the birthright. Therefore, when the time came for Esau to receive his blessing, it was too late. And when Esau heard the words of his father, he cried with a great and exceeding bitter cry, and said unto his father, Bless me, even me also, O my father. And he said, Thy brother came with subtilty, and hath taken away thy blessing. And he said, Is not he rightly named Jacob? for he hath supplanted me these two times: he took away my birthright; and, behold, now he hath taken away my blessing. And he said, Hast thou not reserved a blessing for me? And Isaac answered and said unto Esau, Behold, I have made him thy lord, and all his brethren have I given to him for servants; and with corn and wine have I sustained him: and what shall I do now unto thee, my son? And Esau said unto his father, Hast thou but one blessing, my father? bless me, even me also, O my father. And Esau lifted up his voice, and wept. And Isaac his father answered and said unto him, Behold, thy dwelling shall be the fatness of the earth, and of the dew of heaven from above; and by thy sword shalt thou live, and shalt serve thy brother; and it shall come to pass when thou shalt have the dominion, that thou shalt break his yoke from off thy neck. And Esau hated Jacob because of the blessing wherewith his father blessed him: and Esau said in his heart, The days of mourning for my father are at hand; then will I slay my brother Jacob.- Genesis 27:34-41

His personal failure was counting the holy thing, which was his birthright and blessing as nothing, and chose to satisfy his flesh. He was offended by the actions of his brother, but the offense blinded him to the fact that he failed to honor the blessing. He became angry, wrathful, and full of malice *(bitter)* and developed a desire to kill his brother. He was highly offended.

Watering the Seed - The Emotional Tirade

The emotional tirade waters the seed of offense, causing the roots of bitterness to take form and grow. Bitterness will manifest through your emotions that possess the propensity to affect the people around you, negatively. It is very important to understand why the scripture instructs us first to "follow peace with all men". Not doing so can lead to the destruction of the family, workplace camaraderie, and fellowship with other believers.

Anger

Anger is an overcoming spirit that displays feelings of hostility or displeasure. It is a normal feeling that all of us experience, but out of control, it becomes a tool of the enemy. Satan uses anger to cloud your thinking, and cause you to say things that you cannot take back, and will later regret.

> But now ye also put off all these; anger, wrath, malice, blasphemy, filthy communication out of your mouth. - Colossians 3:8

When anger takes you over, you will manifest these signs:

- Irritable: You are impatient or annoyed over things that normally wouldn't be bothersome.
- Impatient: You become intolerant of the mistakes of others.
- You Stare: You stare at people or stare off with an intense look and penetrating eyes.
- Blasphemous: You speak hurtful words to people and complain almost about everything.
- Superiority: You exercise superiority over people. You want to rule and guide, but you cannot follow. You are always right.

If you read the scripture closely, you will see that anger is a progressive emotion that grows from one state to another. Anger will lead to resentment.

Resentment

Resentment disturbs the spirit by rehearsing and reliving the offensive event in the mind. This is the stage where you began to wish you had said or done something about the issue when it first happened. Here are some signs to look for:

- You find yourself rehearsing the words said to you repeatedly, and then rehearse what you should have said in kind. You entertain an inner war of words in your mind.
- If there is a problem, you take it out on the first person that crosses you.
- You throw yourself into an angry tirade and state of confusion, because the person you resent does not see things your way.

Resentment fuels the anger, which then leads to wrath.

> Be not hasty in thy spirit to be angry: for anger resteth in the bosom of fools. - Ecclesiastes 7:9

Wrath

Wrath is a violent and vengeful behavior that results from anger. It is vindictive and seeks retribution. Wrath will justify violent behavior towards the offender; producing the next phase of indignation which is malice.

Malice

Malice is the strong desire to not just see, but also actually inflict the hurt and pain on the one who trespassed against you. When a person becomes malicious, they perform the violent or revengeful act. Signs of malice are:

- You rejoice at the failures of others.
- You say the failures of others are the result of sin.
- You manipulate people and things to promote yourself and your own agenda.
- You speak wounding words.
- You find it hard to forgive.
- You seek to vindicate yourself.

- You sabotage others dreams by downing them or literally attempt to stop them from achieving.

The next level is not so much as against the trespasser, but against the principles of God. Committing a vengeful act is blasphemy against God.

Blasphemy

Blasphemy is knowing what the will of God is, but choosing to show a great disrespect for what is morally and spiritually right and proceeding in the act of malice. When blasphemy is committed, it lowers the spirit of a person to its most base state resulting in filthy communication. This is also the outward manifestation of a defiled spirit.

Filthy Communication

Filthy communication is more than just cussing. Filthy communication breeds wicked and malicious acts. In this is the power of words. Notice that after bitterness has set in and the act is committed. Filthy words that are associated with lewd behavior become prevalent.

> Even so the tongue is a little member, and boasteth great things. Behold, how great a matter a little fire kindleth! And the tongue is a fire, a world of iniquity: so is the tongue among our members, that it defileth the whole body, and setteth on fire the course of nature; and it is set on fire of hell. For every kind of beasts, and of birds, and of serpents, and of things in the sea, is tamed, and hath been tamed of mankind: But the tongue can no man tame; it is an unruly evil, full of deadly poison. Therewith bless we God, even the Father; and therewith curse we men, which are made after the similitude of God. Out of the same mouth proceedeth blessing and cursing. My brethren, these things ought not so to be. - James 3:5-10

These words fuel the actions, while the act is being committed. These words are proof positive that the person has reached his lowest state.

Personal Failures

Sometimes personal failures are not people oriented or spiritual. Sometimes offense can set in due to life failures in taking advantage of opportunities, even in your current life. Some of these failures involve not going to school and getting that degree, being fired from a job because of irresponsibility or mishandling a relationship that could have gone well, if you had not spoken harsh words or done something rash out of anger. These failures breed the root of bitterness. However, the emotions can run the same course. You can become angry with yourself and fall into resentment, by beating yourself up for not doing what you could have done to make your life or situation better. You punish your mind with negative self-talk, bringing sorrow and depression upon your soul.

Wrath and malice can play a dangerous role on a personal level, because they yield thoughts of suicide as punishment. Suicidal thoughts can come through the feelings of worthlessness and hopelessness because of past failures. Overall, becoming bitter blinds you to the fact of knowing that God is a God of second chances.

The Root Runs Deep

Once these emotions feed into the root system of your heart, the roots break through into the soil of your soul; feeding you different feelings, while blinding you to your own faults in the situation.

Satan uses the root of bitterness, much like the roots of a tree, to store up memories of the offending event; feeding your emotional tirade and using it a means to keep you ensnared. If these feelings are not dealt with immediately, these emotions will soon grow into a tree that will yield fruit, offending everyone and everything around you. This is the meaning of "many being defiled."

Explicit Instruction - Anger and Bitterness

Be ye angry, and sin not: let not the sun go down upon your wrath: Neither give place to the devil. Let him that stole steal no more: but rather let him labour, working with his hands the thing which is good, that he may have to give to him that needeth. Let no corrupt communication proceed out of your mouth, but that which is good to the use of edifying, that it may minister grace unto the hearers. And grieve not the Holy Spirit of God, whereby ye are sealed unto the day of redemption. Let all bitterness, and wrath, and anger, and clamour, and evil speaking, be put away from you, with all malice - Ephesians 4:26-31

Bitterness can affect many areas of your life, your relationships, your health, your drive to live, fear and mental weakness.

Bitterness in Relationships

Because of a bad relationship or a difficult divorce, bitterness can cause you to write people off too quick, even when they are being nice to you. You figure, because one man or woman did you wrong, all are the same way. This closes your mind to being open to new relationships.

You put up barriers; you buffet everyone that tries to get next to you. You even become cynical about other people in their relationships. This attitude could lead you to shut out friends and people who care about you. All of your arguments are centered on you as being correct. Everyone else is wrong. To stay on this track will lead you into a life of loneliness and the snare of misery.

Bitterness in Health

Becoming bitter can increase your chances of physical disease. The stress of bitterness can affect your immune system, making you vulnerable to stress disorders and diseases like high blood pressure.

Bitterness in Family

Bitterness will cause you to hold onto grudges. Even when you are right, the idea of you not being heard, and told that you are right, grieves you. You want to be obeyed. This is the snare of the devil; pride.

Pride will drive you to exalt yourself above your spouse, demanding respect and acknowledgment. It will cause you to add more hurts to the situation. It will cause you say harsh comments and make decisions without the other spouses consent. Bitterness raises your pride level to the extreme, blinding you to the possibility that the other spouse may be hurting also.

Humble Yourself

You know, sometimes as believers, we can feel like we are privileged by God in certain things. Sometimes we can act as if we are without weakness and incapable of being erroneous. Some people are offended because of the truth. When the truth manifests in their lives in a way that proves their weakness, they can become bitter. Consider what happened to Peter:

> Now Peter sat without in the palace: and a damsel came unto him, saying, Thou also wast with Jesus of Galilee. But he denied before them all, saying, I know not what thou sayest. And when he was gone out into the porch, another maid saw him, and said unto them that were there, This fellow was also with Jesus of Nazareth. And again he denied with an oath, I do not know the man. And after a while came unto him they that stood by, and said to Peter, Surely thou also art one of them; for thy speech bewrayeth thee. Then began he to curse and to swear, saying, I know not the man. And immediately the cock crew. And Peter remembered the word of Jesus, which said unto him, Before the cock crow, thou shalt deny me thrice. And he went out, and wept bitterly. - St. Matthew 26:69-74

Jesus told Peter that before the rooster would crow, he would have denied him three times. During his inquiry, Peter fulfilled all the emotions needed to justify him being bitter. In his denial of Jesus Christ, he included oaths, and finally curses, using blasphemies.

A Biblical Example of Bitterness

> And the son of an Israelitish woman, whose father was an Egyptian, went out among the children of Israel: and this son of the Israelitish woman and a man of Israel strove together in the camp; And the Israelitish woman's son blasphemed the name of the LORD, and cursed. And they brought him unto Moses: (and his mother's name was Shelomith, the daughter of Dibri, of the tribe of Dan:) And they put him in ward, that the mind of the LORD might be shewed them. And the LORD spake unto Moses, saying, Bring forth him that hath cursed without the camp; and let all that heard him lay their hands upon his head, and let all the congregation stone him. And thou shalt speak unto the children of Israel, saying, Whosoever curseth his God shall

bear his sin. And he that blasphemeth the name of the LORD, he shall surely be put to death , and all the congregation shall certainly stone him: as well the stranger, as he that is born in the land, when he blasphemeth the name of the LORD, shall be put to death . And he that killeth any man shall surely be put to death. And he that killeth a beast shall make it good; beast for beast. And if a man cause a blemish in his neighbour; as he hath done , so shall it be done to him; Breach for breach, eye for eye, tooth for tooth: as he hath caused a blemish in a man, so shall it be done to him again. And he that killeth a beast, he shall restore it: and he that killeth a man, he shall be put to death. Ye shall have one manner of law, as well for the stranger, as for one of your own country: for I am the LORD your God. And Moses spake to the children of Israel, that they should bring forth him that had cursed out of the camp, and stone him with stones. And the children of Israel did as the LORD commanded Moses.- Leviticus 24:10-23

The young man in this story was offended in the argument with an Israelite man. The Egyptians were accustomed to blaspheming or cursing their gods when their request were not answered, so this young man assumed it upon himself to blaspheme the God of the Israelite man; wanting to hurt him.

This argument drove him to anger (the striving caused a display of hostility or out of control rage). This led him to wrath (he wanted to be vindictive and sought for the opportunity to do so). This led him to malice (which is after knowing what could hurt the Israelite man, he enacted his plan to see him suffer). The acts of malice associated with his blasphemy, showed a great disrespect for God and things sacred. This can even refer to blaspheming a fellow believer.

Accompanied with the blasphemy was filthy communication; he cursed and displayed lewd behavior. God saw and heard this and called for the young man's death before the people so that others would learn not to blaspheme.

The story does not provide the cause of the argument. This story was revealed as a lesson, that striving in arguments with your brother, sister or leader in the church and the family is dangerous, because it leads the offended to do things that could cause a suffering of dire consequences.

In the workplace, because of offenses, you say negative things to other co-workers about the manager or fellow coworkers. The word gets around and causes division and soon you are fired for insubordination and creating a hostile environment in the workplace.

Being offended is the snare that could lead you to unemployment, kicked out of fellowships and into loneliness. However, forgiveness is the key to your deliverance. Stop focusing on the offense. That is a mind cage. Focus on forgiveness. It hurts, but forgiveness is for you.

Unforgiveness

> Then said he unto the disciples, It is impossible but that offences will come: but woe unto him, through whom they come! It were better for him that a millstone were hanged about his neck, and he cast into the sea, than that he should offend one of these little ones. Take heed to yourselves: If thy brother trespass against thee, rebuke him; and if he repent, forgive him. And if he trespass against thee seven times in a day, and seven times in a day turn again to thee, saying, I repent; thou shalt forgive him. And the apostles said unto the Lord, Increase our faith. And the Lord said, If ye had faith as a grain of mustard seed, ye might say unto this sycamine tree, Be thou plucked up by the root, and be thou planted in the sea; and it should obey you. - St. Luke 17:1-6

Here, Jesus likens unforgiveness to the sycamine tree, because its attributes are much like the structure and works of unforgiveness.

Here are some attributes of the sycamine tree:

- It grew a bitter fruit that was hard to eat because of its sharp and unpleasant taste. A bitter person is hard to deal with because of his sharp words and unpleasant character.
- Only the poor purchased the fruit from the sycamine. The poor represent the spiritually wounded and weak who constantly feed on the fruit. Feeding bitter thoughts into their spirit weaken their ability to manifest Christian character.
- The roots of the tree grow deep and wide into the ground, nourishing a large and tall tree to be displayed. Bitterness

takes over a person's spirit and sets roots into the soul, and is revealed through their character.

- Its wood was used to build caskets. It was associated with death. This is the ultimate end for those who eat the fruit of bitterness. It leads to spiritual death.

Unforgiveness is not being able to pardon a person's trespass against you or one's own trespass against self. What makes forgiveness hard is that we do not allow space for error or weakness in others. We put too much trust in our leaders, church family, and the people we look up too. We forget that no matter how anointed, gifted, business minded, loving, or saved, they are, at the end of the day, they are human and subject to error. When these errors manifest against us, we blind ourselves to this truth and only see the error of the person ways.

> And the servant of the Lord must not strive; but be gentle unto all men, apt to teach, patient, In meekness instructing those that oppose themselves; if God peradventure will give them repentance to the acknowledging of the truth; And that they may recover themselves out of the snare of the devil, who are taken captive by him at his will. - 2 Timothy 2:24-26

Arguing and debating the issue clouds your mind through anger and traps you in a bitter feud that if not repented of, leaves you in a state where your life, ministry and goals in Christ cannot be achieved. If God will forgive them, who are you to hold a grudge?

Forgiveness

Forgiving does not immediately come to mind when a person trespasses against you. But unforgiveness becomes apparent around the resentment stage, after anger sets in. In order to follow peace with all men, you have to forgive. Forgiveness is the key to the trap door of the snare of bitterness.

The beautiful thing about forgiveness is that it empowers you to let go of all things negative and evil. Forgiveness is not forgetting or pretending nothing happened. Forgiveness is for you, and it starts with you. Forgiveness is letting go. You let go by humbling yourself and acknowledging your pain, offenses, and failures to God.

> Humble yourselves therefore under the mighty hand of God, that he may exalt you in due time: Casting all your care upon him; for he careth for you. - 1 Peter 5:6-7

Next is to be reconciled with your brother or sister. While being considerate of your own feelings and making sure your spirit is in the right place with God, before any act of reconciliation begins.

> Brethren, if a man be overtaken in a fault, ye which are spiritual, restore such an one in the spirit of meekness; considering thyself, lest thou also be tempted. - Galatians 6:1

If the offense came from a brother, sister or leaders in your fellowship, express your emotions in a non-hurtful and respectful manner. When they respond, try to understand their point of view. Remember, you are there to reconcile. If they seem unreachable or dead to your comments, your job is to forgive, leave the rest to God, and live your life.

Forgive Yourself

One of the most important aspects of forgiveness is forgiving yourself. To forgive yourself is to love yourself. Stop speaking negatively about yourself, Change your way of thinking. Realize that Jesus has forgiven you of all your sins and that you are a new creature in Jesus Christ.

> How much more shall the blood of Christ, who through the eternal Spirit offered himself without spot to God, purge your conscience from dead works to serve the living God? - Hebrews 9:14

Forgiveness through Jesus Christ purges your conscience of those dead works *(past failures)* and allows you to move forward, by giving you a second chance at life. You can still accomplish life goals. You have to forget the past and press forward.

> Brethren, I count not myself to have apprehended but this one thing I do, forgetting those things which are behind, and reaching forth unto those things which are before, I press toward the mark for the prize of the high calling of God in Christ Jesus. - Philippians 3:13-16

Forgiveness is the extra top soil that will smother and overwater the roots of the tree of bitterness, to the point where it withers away and dies. As soon as you begin the healing process, you will be free from the snare. God will begin to heal your relationships, and your spiritual well-being, stress diminishes, and your physical health will spring forward. God has forgiven you, now it's your turn to forgive and live life again.

Chapter Twelve

The Spirit of Infirmity

What is the Spirit of Infirmity?

The scriptures define this spirit as "the spirit of "asthenia" or "infirmity." To be infirm is to be without strength, in body and mind. Infirmities are more than just sickness and disease. They are long-term afflictions that cause continuous suffering and sorrow and can result in spiritual, emotional, and physical weakness.

> The spirit of a man will sustain his infirmity; but a wounded spirit who can bear? - Proverbs 18:4.

Demonic infirmities cause cycles of suffering by breaking down the spirit of a person; crushing their ability to resist. Many avenues can wound a person's spirit:

- Unforgiveness
- Fear
- Bitterness
- Lust
- Anger
- Rejection

These are just a few. These few avenues of emotions cause physical sickness through stress and worry. The one thing they all have in common is that they come as storms of life. Storms will come, but Satan gets in these storms in order to weaken you with an infirm spirit.

Understand that if your spirit is wounded, you will not have the strength to endure sickness and/or disease, if it incurs. This is where the spirit of infirmity comes into play. He works with other demons to keep you in a cycle of affliction or entanglements.

When a person is entangled in constant affliction, they become confused and twisted in complicated situations. As a believer in Jesus Christ, you know that he came to give you life more abundantly. However, because of constant financial difficulty, striving in labor, bills, and social issues, you find yourself stressed and getting sick. You're confused because this is not "life more abundantly". "If he stated that he would supply all your need according to his riches and glory" why are you caught up in the same storm, repeatedly and you know you're doing things right and to the best of your ability. You are starting to lose faith, and the only message you hear is stay in there, God will deliver. However, nothing is happening. The spirit of infirmity may be at work in your life.

> And he was teaching in one of the synagogues on the Sabbath. And, behold, there was a woman which had a spirit of infirmity eighteen years, and was bowed together, and could in no wise lift up herself. And when Jesus saw her, he called her to him, and said unto her, Woman, thou art loosed from thine infirmity. And he laid his hands on her: and immediately she was made straight, and glorified God. And the ruler of the synagogue answered with indignation, because that Jesus had healed on the Sabbath day, and said unto the people, There are six days in which men ought to work: in them therefore come and be healed, and not on the Sabbath day. The Lord then answered him, and said, Thou hypocrite, doth not each one of you on the Sabbath loose his ox or his ass from the stall, and lead him away to watering? And ought not this woman, being a daughter of Abraham, whom Satan hath bound, lo, these eighteen years, be loosed from this bond on the Sabbath day? Luke 13:10-16

The demonic influence upon this woman was a physical attack on her body and mind. As the scripture implied, she did not have the physical strength to lift herself. Jesus diagnosed the source of this woman's sickness as being demonic. It deprived her of strength, causing her to remain in a bowed or curved state for eighteen years.

This woman's deliverance was twofold. First, he cast off the evil spirit by speaking to her mind saying, "woman thou art loosed from thine infirmity." Secondly, he laid hands on her and healed her of the effects the spirit left upon the woman's body.

This type of possession did not mean that she was not saved or that she had done something sinful to bring about the condition. Jesus still acknowledged her as a daughter of Abraham. This type of possession is a "seize," whereas Satan orchestrated a demonic agent to take over this woman's body against her will.

Another example can be found in the story of the man that laid at the pool of Bethesda. There are some differences in the story. However, the healing of this man was different.

The Man at the Pool of Bethesda

> After this there was a feast of the Jews; and Jesus went up to Jerusalem. Now there is at Jerusalem by the sheep market a pool, which is called in the Hebrew tongue Bethesda, having five porches. In these lay a great multitude of impotent folk, of blind, halt, withered, waiting for the moving of the water. For an angel went down at a certain season into the pool, and troubled the water: whosoever then first after the troubling of the water stepped in was made whole of whatsoever disease he had. And a certain man was there, which had an infirmity thirty and eight years. When Jesus saw him lie, and knew that he had been now a long time in that case, he saith unto him, Wilt thou be made whole? The impotent man answered him, Sir, I have no man, when the water is troubled, to put me into the pool: but while I am coming, another steppeth down before me. Jesus saith unto him, Rise, take up thy bed, and walk. And immediately the man was made whole, and took up his bed, and walked: and on the same day was the Sabbath. - St. John 5:1-9

This man had been impotent for thirty-eight years. "Impotent" comes from "astheneo" which means to be powerless in the ability to take action; helpless or lack sufficient strength or life. His situation was not much different from the woman, except for the symptoms. Note that Jesus started asking probing questions concerning his ailment saying, "wilt thou be made whole?"

Many have taught that the impotent man began to make an excuse as to why he never made it to the pool, not so. The man did possess a faith. He went to this pool around the season that the angel would trouble the waters for thirty-eight years. However, each year, he failed at getting in before someone else would enter. The reason, not an excuse for him not getting in the pool, in time, was due to his bodily impotency.

> The impotent man answered him, Sir, I have no man, when the water is troubled, to put me into the pool: but while I am coming, another steppeth down before me.-St. John 5:7

He was making an effort. His story signified a mental malady of hopelessness because of helplessness caused by his sickness. Yet, he had perseverance, because he went to the pool for thirty-eight years. This is what got Jesus attention, causing to him to ask the question.

Now look at what Jesus did. He spoke a command to the man, as he did the woman with the infirmity saying, "take up thy bed and walk." These were words again spoken to the mind.

In each case, one cannot doubt that these individuals were not only bound by spirits, but were also depressed and sorrowful. Their minds had to be restored. They were spiritually wounded because of their conditions.

Revealing the Snare

In the case of the man at the pool, Jesus warned him to stop sinning or a worse thing would come upon him *(v14)*. The woman with the issue was a daughter of Abraham, who already had her sins forgiven. This man was told not sin anymore. He was explicitly warned that if he went back into sin, possibly the disease or something worse would come upon him.

When people suffer severe illnesses like these two individuals, they adjust to the demands of the illness by sacrificing certain abilities that could positively affect their way of life. Such abilities sacrificed are mobility and, independence. The social life is hampered, financial opportunities are missed, financial burdens begin to mount because of medical bills and so forth. Consider the woman with the issue of blood who spent all her living trying to find a cure for her ailment. The length of these ailments in any person's life is enough to cause depression to set in.

Satan's Opportunity

When a person accepts a sickness or disease as a way of life, the sadness or hopelessness associated with not finding a remedy, gives Satan and his evil minions opportunity to exploit those emotions and use them as a way to increase the strength of the malady and control the victims thought life; sending them into a state of oppression.

> How God anointed Jesus of Nazareth with the Holy Ghost and with power: who went about doing good, and healing all that were oppressed of the devil; for God was with him. - Acts 10:38

The spirit of infirmity magnifies human, spiritual and mental weakness and sickness; resulting in constant cycles of sorrow and suffering which leads to oppression In Acts 10:38, "Oppression" comes from the Greek word "katadunasteuo" which means to exercise cruel or unjust dominion or power over a person, place or thing.

Oppression Causes Depression

When Satan oppresses a person with sickness, he has to take their mind, by locking them down in severe and persistent sadness. A depressed spirit will begin to manifest itself through frustrations, loss of interest in life and activities, loss of sleep *(sleep deprivation mingled with heavy burdens leads to satanic mind control)*, restlessness, irritability, being indecisive and having thoughts of suicide.

Demonic Influence in Sickness

In the ministry of Jesus, you will find that when he worked miracles of healing; casting out demons was also associated with these miracles.

Reference#1

> And he arose out of the synagogue, and entered into Simon's house. And Simon's wife's mother was taken with a great fever; and they besought him for her. And he stood over her, and

rebuked the fever; and it left her: and immediately she arose and ministered unto them. Now when the sun was setting, all they that had any sick with divers diseases brought them unto him; and he laid his hands on every one of them, and healed them. And devils also came out of many, crying out, and saying, Thou art Christ the Son of God. And he rebuking them suffered them not to speak: for they knew that he was Christ. - St. Luke 4:38-41

Reference #2

When the even was come, they brought unto him many that were possessed with devils: and he cast out the spirits with his word, and healed all that were sick: hat it might be fulfilled which was spoken by Esaias the prophet, saying, Himself took our infirmities, and bare our sicknesses.- St. Matthew 8:16-17

Sin and death are intertwined with sickness and disease. Now, this does not mean that if a person is sick, it's because of sin, but it is the result of humankind's fall from grace into sin. The bible describes many sicknesses as being a result of demonic possession. For example:

Epilepsy

Known symptoms of this disease are convulsions or seizures that involve an extreme shaking, staring off, or frequent daydreaming. In some cases, there is a hard stiffening or jerking of the body, lip smacking, chewing and fidgeting. After some seizures, the victim can suffer memory loss or loss of consciousness. Now let's look at the scripture:

And, behold, a man of the company cried out, saying, Master, I beseech thee, look upon my son: for he is mine only child. And, lo, a spirit taketh him, and he suddenly crieth out; and it teareth him that he foameth again, and bruising him hardly departeth from him. And I besought thy disciples to cast him out; and they could not. And Jesus answering said, O faithless and perverse generation, how long shall I be with you, and suffer you? Bring thy son hither. And as he was yet a coming, the devil threw him down, and tare him. And Jesus rebuked the unclean spirit, and healed the child, and delivered him again to his father. - St. Luke 9:42

The word "teareth" comes from "sparasso" which means to convulse or tear with epilepsy. Sparasso is connected to the English word "spasm" which is an uncontrollable tightening or hard contraction of the muscles. "Foameth" has two meanings. The first is "aphrizo" which mean to froth or produce bubbles out of the mouth and the second is "qetseph" which indicates rage.

In St. Mark 9:18, there is another symptom called "pineth" or "pineth away. To pine away is to "xeraino" which means to shrivel or lose vigor, strength, or health in the body. Other symptoms in St. Mark 9:22, states that the unclean spirit caused him to attempt acts of suicide, by trying to make him drown himself or burn himself with fire. When Jesus asked the father, "When did these events start? The father responded, "Since he was a child." Children are the main victims of epilepsy. Epilepsy in the scriptures is demonic in nature.

Obedience, Sickness & Communion

Now, not all diseases are associated with sin. However, if sickness is a factor in your life, then you should consider one more reason: Disobedience and self-deception.

Righteous living is a serious commandment for Gods people. However, we are living in a time where teachings are coming forth, telling people that "no matter what they do, they can't lose their salvation. Teachings that justify sin are traps in which many have been led into. Read the instruction given to Timothy:

> Nevertheless, the foundation of God standeth sure, having this seal, The Lord knoweth them that are his. And, Let every one that nameth the name of Christ depart from iniquity. - 2 Timothy 2:19

This scripture challenges us to examine ourselves to see if we are really in the faith. This examination comes in two ways: by looking into the word and the taking of communion.

> For I have received of the Lord that which also I delivered unto you, that the Lord Jesus the same night in which he was betrayed took bread: And when he had given thanks, he brake it, and said, Take, eat: this is my body, which is broken for you: this do in remembrance of me. After the same manner also he took the cup,

when he had supped, saying, this cup is the new testament in my blood: this do ye, as oft as ye drink it, in remembrance of me. For as often as ye eat this bread, and drink this cup, ye do shew the Lord's death till he come. Wherefore whosoever shall eat this bread, and drink this cup of the Lord, unworthily, shall be guilty of the body and blood of the Lord. But let a man examine himself, and so let him eat of that bread, and drink of that cup. For he that eateth and drinketh unworthily, eateth and drinketh damnation to himself, not discerning the Lord's body. For this cause many are weak and sickly among you, and many sleep. - 2 Corinthians 11:23-30

Many in the church world have participated in the taking of communion, without purging their lives of iniquities. Doing so has caused a sweep of sickness and disease throughout the church and the world. A religious spirit of deception has executed this plan through false teachers.

To take communion unworthily, is to take it with an unconverted heart and irreverent spirit. This is a terrible sin against the Lord, because taking communion means that you walk in total respect of Christ's crucifixion and its purpose and receive the benefits of his work. To live in sin or have iniquity in the heart such as lust, bitterness, or unforgiveness, is being guilty of the body and blood. This brings about damnation through sickness, weakness, and death.

Obedience

Verily, verily, I say unto you, He that believeth on me hath everlasting life. I am that bread of life. Your fathers did eat manna in the wilderness, and are dead. This is the bread which cometh down from heaven, that a man may eat thereof, and not die. I am the living bread which came down from heaven: if any man eat of this bread, he shall live forever: and the bread that I will give is my flesh, which I will give for the life of the world. The Jews therefore strove among themselves, saying, How can this man give us his flesh to eat? Then Jesus said unto them, Verily, verily, I say unto you, Except ye eat the flesh of the Son of man, and drink his blood, ye have no life in you. Whoso eateth my flesh, and drinketh my blood, hath eternal life; and I will raise him up at the last day. For my flesh is meat indeed, and my blood is drink indeed. He that eateth my flesh, and drinketh my blood, dwelleth in me, and I in him. As the living Father hath sent me, and I live by the Father: so he that eateth me, even he shall live by me. This is that bread which came down from heaven: not as your fathers did eat manna, and are dead: he that eateth of this bread shall live forever. - St. John 6:47-58

After Jesus said these words, many of the disciples left him, because they misunderstood the meaning. Jesus was not speaking of cannibalism; he was speaking of obedience to his word. If they were obedient, they would be able to experience an enriched life in Christ, devoted to God.

He was speaking of fellowship and knowing him in a relationship, not just in words. He used a similitude where he likened himself to bread consumed. In Matthew 4:4, he states that, "man cannot live by bread alone, but by every word out of the mouth of God." In these scriptures, we see the meaning of communion. Jesus was simply speaking of devotion to the words he spoke.

If you have sin or iniquity in your life, and are suffering constant sickness or disease, your deliverance may just lie in the simple task of repenting of the sin and submitting yourself to the obedience of God's word. Then you can take communion. After all, it is a requirement for you and all believers. It shows that you have the life of Christ in you and it qualifies you for heaven.

Verily, verily, I say unto you, Except ye eat the flesh of the Son of man, and drink his blood, ye have no life in you. Whoso eateth my flesh, and drinketh my blood, hath eternal life; and I will raise him up at the last day. - St. John 6:53-54

Repent and break free of these satanic snares by submitting yourself to obeying the word of God.

Section III

Tools for Deliverance

Chapter Thirteen

Can A Christian Be Demon Possessed?

There is a great concern about demon possession in the mind of Christians. The concern has created a question that has been asked numerous times in bible studies, pastoral counsels, and articles. The question is "can a Christian be demon possessed? When you study the scriptures, and understand the character of God, Jesus Christ, and The power of the Holy Spirit and compare them to the nature of Satan, his demons and the anti-spirit and how they operate in contrast with one another, the answer to the question is "absolutely, positively, No!"

This question does not arise as a random thought. This question is rooted in fear, the fear of being possessed. Truth be told, this question comes up constantly in the mind of a person who has iniquity or secret sin in their lives that they cannot stop or will not stop committing. Their idea of what demon possession looks like comes from Hollywood horror films and brimstone sermons. However, demon possession can be much milder but most deceitful and dangerous than what is portrayed in films. Demon possession is revealed in the character and acts of sin that one commits.

Understanding Possession

When you purchase a home, ownership is transferred from the seller to the buyer. Once the purchaser has paid the "price," the new owner has the legal right, which is sealed with his signature, to take control of the house and occupy it. Once the owner is in the residence, he is able to manipulate the inside of that home to suit his likings. Any other form of possession would be considered an invasion, domination, and unlawful occupation of a property against the "will of the owner.

Therefore, possession signifies ownership. Ownership comes through occupation, providing control. The owner of the property, by law, has the right to do whatever he wants with the property, even distribute duties of work over the property and divide ownership by percentages to other entities.

The Purchased Possession

> In whom also we have obtained an inheritance, being predestinated according to the purpose of him who worketh all things after the counsel of his own will: That we should be to the praise of his glory, who first trusted in Christ. In whom ye also trusted, after that ye heard the word of truth, the gospel of your salvation: in whom also after that ye believed, ye were sealed with that Holy Spirit of promise, Which is the earnest of our inheritance until the redemption of the purchased possession, unto the praise of his glory. – Ephesians 1:11-14

According to the scriptures, when you accepted Jesus Christ as your Lord, and Savior through the gospel, your faith "sealed" you with the "Spirit of promise." When Jesus died on the cross, and descended into the lower parts of the earth, he paid the sin debt in full *(1 Corinthians 7:23)*. He took upon himself the full punishment for all the sins of humanity, satisfying God's wrath, and righteous judgment against you.

"Sealed" comes from the Greek term "sphragizo," meaning stamped with a signet for security or preservation. Webster's dictionary defines a signet as "a seal used to officially give personal authority to a document, *(in this case, transfer of ownership from Satan to Jesus Christ, satisfying the Judgment of God)* in place of the signature. That seal is the "Spirit of Promise."

The moment you repented of your sins and accepted Jesus Christ, the regeneration of your mind and character began through the spirit of God.

This only would I learn of you, Received ye the Spirit by the works of the law, or by the hearing of faith? - Galatians 3:2

The seal is not only a signet of protection; it is a mark of identity. The mark of God is the change in your character and life that will identify you as a member of the "purchased possession," the church of Jesus Christ *(Acts 20:28)*. Through his sacrifice, he signed the writ of execution against you *(Romans 6:23)*, taking possession of your soul, and occupying your mind and life, with The Holy Spirit. It is the Holy Spirit of God, like the occupants of a new home changing the interior for suitable living, begins to change your life and way of thinking.

Accepting Jesus Christ through the gospel of faith and being filled with the Holy Spirit breaks the yokes of sin *(the law of Satan)* and bondage *(the works of demons)* from over your life. Because you have a new owner, the course of life that you will now live is according to the word of God. That is totally contrary to the law of sin and power of Satan.

> And you hath he quickened, who were dead in trespasses and sins; Wherein in time past ye walked according to the course of this world, according to the prince of the power of the air, the spirit that now worketh in the children of disobedience: Among whom also we all had our conversation in times past in the lusts of our flesh, fulfilling the desires of the flesh and of the mind; and were by nature the children of wrath, even as others. But God, who is rich in mercy, for his great love wherewith he loved us, Even when we were dead in sins, hath quickened us together with Christ, (by grace ye are saved;)- Ephesians 2:1-5

According to Revelation 3:20, Jesus is standing and knocking at the door of the unbeliever's heart, and calling him to a better life here on earth and eternal life in the end.

The Children of Disobedience

The children of disobedience, the unsaved are demon possessed, but not to the degree that the Hollywood films portray. Demon possession operates on different levels and through "persistent disobedience" to the will of God. In Ephesians 2:2, take note of the term "worketh" which is interpreted from the Greek term "energeo" meaning an active supernatural power that energizes unbelievers to live in disobedience to the word of God.

This type of possession is limited to its effects in a person's life. The degree of possession here is the result of Adam's fall in the Garden of Eden. All men after Adam was born into sin and *(spiritually)* shaped in iniquity.

> The wicked are estranged from the womb: they go astray as soon as they be born, speaking lies. – Psalms 58:3

As men, we are born into disobedience. We are born with a sin nature. However, the devil has limits to what he can do, even in a sinner's life. If God had not set limits, from the womb, all of humanity would have entered this world foaming and maniacal.

The Legal Rights

According to Revelation 3:20, Jesus stands at that door of our hearts, knocking, and appealing to us to follow him, It is when we accept him as Lord that he will come into our hearts, live in us, and steer our path through his intelligence and power. We have to give Jesus legal right to do so. Satan and his demons operate in the same manner. Satan knocks at the door of our hearts, tempting us with the sinful things we enjoy. If we give way to the temptation, we give him the legal right to enter into our hearts and like Christ, direct us in unrighteousness through the power of sin, which are demonic forces. Whatever voice we yield to determines who has the advantage of over our life and mind

> Know ye not, that to whom ye yield yourselves servants to obey, his servants ye are to whom ye obey; whether of sin unto death, or of obedience unto righteousness?- Romans 6:16.

The only way a demon can take possession of a Christian is for him give up his salvation by going back into persistent sin. When this happens, he is no longer a Christian. He became a slave to the bondages of sin, which will ultimately lead to spiritual, and if not repented of, eternal death in hell.

He that committeth sin is of the devil; for the devil sinneth from the beginning. For this purpose the Son of God was manifested, that he might destroy the works of the devil. Whosoever is born of God doth not commit sin; for his seed remaineth in him: and he cannot sin, because he is born of God. In this the children of God are manifest, and the children of the devil: whosoever doeth not righteousness is not of God, neither he that loveth not his brother. - 1 John 3:8-10

Demons have to have a doorway of legal entrance into your life. They cannot override your free will. If you engage in watching pornography, the porn is the doorway that allows the lustful spirit access. Committing the act gives it permission to take over your thoughts. It then keeps you pre-occupied with the thoughts of satisfying your flesh. If you are involved in the occult, the usage of Ouija boards, satanic symbolism or witchcraft can open doors to chronic demonic possession. Remaining bitter opens doors to demonic possession. Anger and resentment are keys that unlock the door for entrance into your spirit.

All acts of sin are doorways that allow demons to enter in and take possession. The sin itself is what feeds the growth of the evil spirit. The more the acts are committed, the greater the need to commit the act grows. This is why constantly engaging in lust, can lead to more severe acts of satisfaction. The demonic spirit will lead a person to move from one extreme to the next.

Sin, which is the laws of Satan, provides the legal rights for demons to control of your life. Let's look at some of its forms:

"Avown" means moral evil. It signifies an intentional perverted life, a justifying of wrongdoing: Iniquity.
"Hamartia" means missing the mark or sin against God by transgressing or going beyond the limits.
"Adikia" means wickedness (being evil) or injustice (unfair)
"Anomia" is defying the law of God.

All these acts are selfish acts that man must fall into purposely, giving demons access to his mind to be manipulated. This is why you must; bring your body under subjection to the word of God through praying and fasting. You have to stop sinning. Stopping the sin will close the doors. Heed this stern warning:

Nevertheless the foundation of God standeth sure, having this seal, The Lord knoweth them that are his. And, let every one that nameth the name of Christ depart from iniquity. – 2 Timothy 2:19

The Deceitfulness of the Trap

You do not want to be caught in a cycle of committing the same sin repeatedly or attempting to ride pity for yourself, thinking that God will sympathize with you and let you into heaven. The deceitfulness of the trap is that these demon spirits will cause you to think that you're hurting because you are righteous or maybe bad things are just happening to a good person. The purpose of a trap is to catch you and hold you, until Jesus returns and finds you in a bound state. By that time, it will be too late. The second purpose of the trap is contain you, bleed out all righteousness, and soon destroy you.

You cannot be a Christian, bound in sin. The only way sin is working in your life is because you're feeding it through its various avenues. You may be bitter because someone offended you, but the trap is to keep you angry and resentful, focusing on the offense and harboring unforgiveness. Rejection is an identity problem, you have to raise yourself in the word, or it will lead you into low-esteem and doubt, which brings about damnation. Lust is prevalent in your life because you feed pornography to your spirit. Sickness is not sinful, but if you are partaking in communion unworthily, you strengthen the spirit of infirmity in your life. You have to make a change and be willing to let things go. Sin does not draw Gods sympathy.

In the next chapter, I will give you some tools that you can apply immediately and break free. God has not forsaken you. This is your time for deliverance.

Chapter Fourteen

Spiritual Weapons: Part 1 Breaking Strongholds

(For the weapons of our warfare are not carnal, but mighty through God to the pulling down of strong holds ;) Casting down imaginations, and every high thing that exalteth itself against the knowledge of God, and bringing into captivity every thought to the obedience of Christ; And having in a readiness to revenge all disobedience, when your obedience is fulfilled. - 2 Corinthians 10:4-6

Paul was under constant attack by men, who were false apostles and deceivers that challenged his apostleship and character. Paul boldly addressed their accusations and evil works in his letters. However, he chose to engage in warfare against their works using spiritual weapons instead of natural means.

The more effort you make in living and striving to live holy, Satan, your accuser, will always find ways to execute attempts at manipulating your will to his, by challenging your faith, slandering your character and tempting you to act out of the will of God.

Like Paul, you must not meet the devil on his terms. You have to use spiritual weapons, which are mighty through God.

Grow Strong in the Lord

Finally, my brethren, be strong in the Lord, and in the power of his might. - Ephesians 6:10

Here, Paul explicitly states where your strength should come from. In order for you to be strong in the Lord, you must walk in the same power that Jesus did, and that power comes from the Holy Ghost and obedience to will of God.

Before Jesus began his earthly ministry, he went to the river Jordan to be baptized by John, the Baptist. After he was baptized, the spirit of God descended from heaven and rested on him, empowering him to go forth and overcome the temptations of Satan in the wilderness.

Jesus Baptism

> The Spirit of the Lord GOD is upon me; because the LORD hath anointed me to preach good tidings unto the meek; he hath sent me to bind up the brokenhearted, to proclaim liberty to the captives, and the opening of the prison to them that are bound; To proclaim the acceptable year of the LORD, and the day of vengeance of our God; to comfort all that mourn; To appoint unto them that mourn in Zion, to give unto them beauty for ashes, the oil of joy for mourning, the garment of praise for the spirit of heaviness; that they might be called trees of righteousness, the planting of the LORD, that he might be glorified.- Isaiah 61:1-3

The Holy Ghost empowered Jesus to carry out the will of the Father by destroying the works and bondages of sin and Satan off the lives of men. Isaiah 11:1-4, describes the knowledge and wisdom that he would use through the spirit of God to make righteous judgments in counsel and reproof.

> After he was baptized, he fasted for forty days. The Spirit of God then led him into the wilderness to be tempted by the devil. Every temptation that Jesus experienced, he overcame it by quoting the word of God (St. Luke 4:1-13).

When the temptations ended, Jesus started his ministry by preaching the gospel, casting out devils, healing the sick, and engaging the false religious system of the Pharisees through his deeds and holy character, bringing them to an open shame.

Take note of this fact: during the tenure of his ministry, Jesus, after he would work a miracle, would retire into seclusion to pray.

Afterwards, he would come forth and work more miracles before the people and the disciples.

As a child of God, you must follow the same pattern that Jesus did in order to be empowered over the works of the enemy. You must:

- Experience the baptism of the Holy Ghost: *(Acts 1:8)*
- Fast: Isaiah 58:5-14; St. Luke 5:33-35
- Pray often: St. Luke 18:1; Ephesians 6:18
- Study *(obey)* The Word: 2 Timothy 2:15; Ephesians 6:17

All of these Jesus did, which enabled him to defeat the powers of the enemy through the Spirit of God. If you revisit St. Luke 4:1-13, you will notice that the first temptation was geared towards his flesh; the second and third temptations were geared towards his mind, Satan did the same thing to eve; he planted a thought in her mind, which then changed her perceptions of the tree and the commands of God.

All of the attributes of Jesus anointing in Isaiah 11:1-5, deals with thoughts *(the mind)* and righteousness *(the word)*. To walk in the power of Jesus might is be baptized with the Holy Ghost and taking on the same mind of Christ, which is obedience to the word of God.

This brings us to the idea of strongholds.

Strongholds

I was hoping that you would see a common theme throughout this book as it relates to each demonic force. The common theme is that every temptation works in your mind. Your spirit is your mind or your heart, it is the seat of your character, your emotions, and it is the center of your morals, thoughts, imaginations, perceptions, understandings, and reasoning's. The word 'heart" comes from the Greek word "kardia" which is figurative for thoughts and feelings. If the devil can hold your mind, he can control you.

Webster's dictionary defines strongholds as "a fortified place dominated by a particular group *(demons)* or marked by a particular characteristic *(Lust and masturbation, rejection and bitterness, anger and wrath, etc...)*. The Greek word is "ochuroma" which means to "fortify as if by holding." It is figurative of an argument.

Therefore, strongholds are mental fortresses of practiced ideas, thoughts, and characteristics, erected by demonic forces. Strongholds can also be defined as mind prisons that hold demonic influences that manipulate and control a person's will, keeping them from carrying out the plan of God in their lives.

Whenever you suffer a traumatic, offensive, or immoral event, the enemy uses those events to establish mind prisons that will hold those thoughts and use them to keep you from moving forward in the Lord. These strongholds are formed through imaginations.

Imaginations

Imaginations are mental images and concepts that connect to your senses and fleshly desires. If you smell an aroma of baked bread, you imagine the image in your mind of what it looks like, fresh out of the oven. This triggers, a mouth-watering effect, which then creates a desire for you to find the source of the aroma and indulge yourself. You have been driven to go taste. You have to have it. You deter from your destination, make time to stop at that bakery and make your purchase.

Imagination of sin works the same way. They are consistent with your reality and your own reasoning, for pursuing pleasure, while justifying the pursuit. Imaginations justify wrongdoing and lead men to develop a dark mind.

> Because that, when they knew God, they glorified him not as God, neither were thankful; but became vain in their imaginations, and their foolish heart was darkened. - Romans 1:21

Evil Imaginations are tools of satanic temptations that are designed to distract you away from the strait path of holiness. These evil imaginations are connected to "your own desires" that must be crucified and brought under subjection to the word of God.

The High Thing That Exalts Itself

The next thing that strengthens the imagination in your mind is the high thing. The high thing exalts itself against the knowledge or the word of God. Now refer back to Paul's words to the Roman church *(Romans 1:21)*. The people's hearts were darkened because of their evil imaginations. However, here is something to consider. *They knew God, but did not glorify him as God,* meaning that they did not submit to the authority of His word.

The key words here are "exalts itself." The high thing is a living thing that exalts or raises itself up against the word of God, using its own ideas as the law, justifying the action to be committed. The high thing is your "determined action and decision to indulge the imagination "knowing that the act is against the word of God.

This was the snare of Lucifer, which caused him to become Satan. He exalted himself by yielding to his own desire. *(Isaiah 14:13)*. The high thing is the willingness to be disobedient. Note Paul's words in the scripture:

> ...bringing into captivity every thought to the obedience of Christ; And having in a readiness to revenge all disobedience, when your obedience is fulfilled (2 Corinthians 10:5-6)

You have to be willing to submit yourself to the authority of God's word and stop being a willing slave to sin. You have to take revenge against all disobedience by obeying the scripture. Strongholds are broken by resisting the devil when he magnifies evil thoughts *(imaginations or reasons why you should do a thing)* that appeal to your desires. Doing so will cause him to flee from you.

The Outward Appearance of a Thing

> Do ye look on things after the outward appearance? if any man trust to himself that he is Christ's, let him of himself think this again, that, as he is Christ's, even so are we Christ's.-2 Corinthians 10:7

The outward appearances of things seem innocent and enticing. Again, you have to change your thinking and view things from the standpoint of God's word. In the case of bitterness, remember what Gods word says about it. In the case of materialism, remember what Gods word says. When an enticement is presented, you have to think righteously. This is why Apostle Paul asked the question in verse 7.

The danger behind yielding, while knowing what the word of God says, and not use it as a defense against temptation, but as a means to justify yielding, is to establish your own righteousness. You do what you think is right or feel is right. You have to use righteous judgment in order to break the stronghold.

> Judge not according to the appearance, but judge righteous judgment.-St. John 7:24

This is why Paul chose to use his spiritual weapons against his enemies in the church of Corinth. They were more effective and guaranteed to gain victories over his opposition. Paul submitted himself to the authority of scripture and the power of the Holy Ghost in order to break the satanic influence that was working against him, through those men in the church at Corinth.

Chapter Fifteen

Spiritual Weapons: Part 2: The Armor of God

Stand therefore, having your loins girt about with truth, and having on the breastplate of righteousness; And your feet shod with the preparation of the gospel of peace; Above all, taking the shield of faith, wherewith ye shall be able to quench all the fiery darts of the wicked. And take the helmet of salvation, and the sword of the Spirit, which is the word of God: Praying always with all prayer and supplication in the Spirit, and watching thereunto with all perseverance and supplication for all saints;- Ephesians 6:14-18

The purpose of the spiritual armor is give you strength against the enemy and the ability to stand firm in the day of testing. Spiritual battles are manifested through human interactions, in the home, the family, the workplace, and any other areas that effect our social lives. These battles are not be fought by fleshly means.

Apostle Paul; wanted the church at Ephesus to understand that the churches persecution and tests of trials were a result of the demon spirits being stirred and angry because of their three year residency in Ephesus; preaching the word of kingdom and bringing there pagan practices to an open shame.

Note that every piece of armor is constructed by the word of God. The reason for this is to remind you that the battle is not yours; it is the Lords.

Loins Girded with Truth

> Wherefore gird up the loins of your mind, be sober, and hope to the end for the grace that is to be brought unto you at the revelation of Jesus Christ;-1 Peter 1:13

Having your loins girded with truth signifies "uprightness and readiness" in the word of God; prepared to engage all temptations that try to impede your progress in the Lord. The belt wrapped around the loins of the soldier and held the sword and scabbard. The most important operation of the belt was that it held all the armor pieces together.

How dangerous would it be for a soldier to run into battle without his sword and his gear, not properly held together? The same goes for facing temptation without knowing the truth of God's word.

> Study to shew thyself approved unto God, a workman that needeth not to be ashamed, rightly dividing the word of truth.-2 Timothy 2:15

Being ready, is remaining focused on the road to fulfilling your purpose and destiny. It's being aware of the devils devices, whether they are predictable or uncertain. Remember, your adversary is as roaring lion seeking to destroy you *(1 Peter 5:8)*.

Then there is uprightness. Being upright indicates the idea of always walking in the truth of God's word, taking heed to your ways, and how you live among those who are not saved. The world should see the light of Christ in you and feel the influence of his power emanating from your spirit. This will stir contrary people against you, and even brethren to challenge you and your faith. Be ready to revenge all disobedience that tempts you with the word of God.

> Let your loins be girded about, and your lights burning;-St. Luke 12:35

The Breastplate of Righteousness

> But let us, who are of the day, be sober, putting on the breastplate of faith and love; and for an helmet, the hope of salvation. - 1 Thessalonians 5:8

The breastplate of righteousness is a symbol of obedience through faith and love. It holds the idea of trusting God's word to be effective in the face of temptation and doing what is right.

> If ye know that he is righteous, ye know that every one that doeth righteousness is born of him.-1 John 2:29

The breastplate of the soldier's armor was designed to protect the vital organs within the torso. Without a breastplate, a soldier entering battle was as good as dead. Righteousness was also a symbol that represented the battle skills and maneuvers of the soldier in the face of temptation. It represented the knowledge and active wisdom in battle.

> Riches profit not in the day of wrath: but righteousness delivereth from death. - Proverbs 11:4

Love for God is more than just lip service. To love God is to obey His commands and trust His guidance in situations that seem undefeatable. Obedience in doing what is right is to exercise faith through your works when temptation presents itself.

> Awake to righteousness, and sin not; for some have not the knowledge of God: I speak this to your shame.-1 Corinthians 15:34

Keeping the commandments of Jesus Christ is necessary for saving faith and preserving your soul for eternal life. Your obedience must be real, not a display of emotionalism.

> He that hath my commandments, and keepeth them, he it is that loveth me: and he that loveth me shall be loved of my Father, and I will love him, and will manifest myself to him. - St. John 14:21

Shoes Prepared With the Gospel of Peace

> How then shall they call on him in whom they have not believed? and how shall they believe in him of whom they have not heard? and how shall they hear without a preacher? And how shall they preach, except they be sent? as it is written, How beautiful are the feet of them that preach the gospel of peace, and bring glad tidings of good things!-Romans 10:14-15

The soldier's shoes allowed him to walk on hard and rough terrains, enabling him to walk without stumbling. During battle, the right shoes helped him to watch his footing; providing confidence and stability while facing enemy threats. Having the right shoes allowed the soldier to go forth and accomplish his mission.

Your spiritual shoes will allow you to go forth as a witness of the power of God. It is here that you will gain the confidence in walking in your purpose and destiny, which is eternal life without the worry of stumbling.

> He that loveth his brother abideth in the light, and there is none occasion of stumbling in him. - 1 John 2:10

In your spiritual journey, you will come across many people that will attempt to offend you, persecute you, and harm you. The peace of God will remind you of who your enemy is and keep you in control of your emotions.

> Follow peace with all men, and holiness, without which no man shall see the Lord:-Hebrews 12:14

In the face of temptations, your feet shod with the preparation of the gospel of peace will keep you focused on your mission, which is to continue spreading the gospel through your life and message.

The Shield of Faith

> If it be so, our God whom we serve is able to deliver us from the burning fiery furnace, and he will deliver us out of thine hand, O king. But if not, be it known unto thee, O king, that we will not serve thy gods, nor worship the golden image which thou hast set up. Then was Nebuchadnezzar full of fury, and the form of his

visage was changed against Shadrach, Meshach, and Abednego: therefore he spake, and commanded that they should heat the furnace one seven times more than it was wont to be heated. And he commanded the most mighty men that were in his army to bind Shadrach, Meshach, and Abednego, and to cast them into the burning fiery furnace. Then these men were bound in their coats, their hosen, and their hats, and their other garments, and were cast into the midst of the burning fiery furnace. Therefore because the king's commandment was urgent, and the furnace exceeding hot, the flames of the fire slew those men that took up Shadrach, Meshach, and Abednego. And these three men, Shadrach, Meshach, and Abednego, fell down bound into the midst of the burning fiery furnace. Then Nebuchadnezzar the king was astonished, and rose up in haste, and spake, and said unto his counsellors, Did not we cast three men bound into the midst of the fire? They answered and said unto the king, True, O king. He answered and said, Lo, I see four men loose, walking in the midst of the fire, and they have no hurt; and the form of the fourth is like the Son of God.- Daniel 3:17-25

The story of the three Hebrew boys is a perfect example of how the shield of faith works. The shield is not a part of the body armor of the soldier. It is a defensive tool, which must be taken up, and used to block or shield oneself from the strikes and arrows of the opponent. The design of the shield, especially for a Roman soldier, was a long, rectangular shaped, but curved around the edges. The soldier, during battle, would raise the shield to block barrages of arrows or wild, swinging blows from the enemy. The shield was long enough to cover almost the entire body when used.

When the Hebrew boys were faced with death for not bowing down to a false god image, it was at the moment, that they raised their shield of faith against the enemy. The shield was raised through these words:

If it be so, our God whom we serve is able to deliver us from the burning fiery furnace, and he will deliver us out of thine hand, O king. But if not, be it known unto thee, O king, that we will not serve thy gods, nor worship the golden image which thou hast set up.-Daniel 7:17-18

They had enough faith to believe that God would save them, either before, during or after their time in the fiery furnace and if God, had not done so, they believed that he was well able to do it. The shield was working when they were tossed in. They went into the fire bound in all their clothing and was found by the king walking around in the fire with the Son of God. When they came forth from the furnace, not only were they not burned, they did not bear the scent of the fire, nor where they singed. Therefore, as the Roman shield was designed to cover the entire body, the shield faith, covered the Hebrew Boys while in the fiery furnace.

> For we are saved by hope: but hope that is seen is not hope: for what a man seeth, why doth he yet hope for? But if we hope for that we see not, then do we with patience wait for it.-Romans 8:24-25

The shield of faith will ward off any attacks from the enemy, while you wait for God's deliverance. Some battles may become highly intense and fiery, like the heat of the furnace being magnified seven times hotter for the Hebrew Boys. These kinds of battles Satan fires off darts of worry, fear, and doubt. It is during these times that you must raise your shield, by trusting in the Lord, hoping and waiting for your deliverance.

> Now faith is the substance of things hoped for, the evidence of things not seen. - Hebrews 11:1

Your faith stands in place of the thing that you need God to bless you with. If your trouble is economical, your faith stands in place of the monies you need. If you need healing from sickness or disease, your faith stands at the object of the thing not seen. You're simply waiting for your deliverance to manifest through faith.

The Helmet of Salvation

> But let us, who are of the day, be sober, putting on the breastplate of faith and love; and for an helmet, the hope of salvation. - 1 Thessalonians 5:8

The helmet of salvation was designed to protect the soldiers head, during battle. To the believer, the helmet is an assurance of salvation and deliverance. The helmet is taking on the mind of Christ, which protects us from the cares of this world.

Spiritual warfare is a mind battle. In order to remain vigilant, we have to remain sober and watchful. In the heat of the battle, a soldier could lose focus and panic because of the chaos happening around him. When Peter stepped out of the ship to go and meet Jesus on waters, the boisterous winds, and waves caused him to lose focus on Jesus and he began to sink. Peter knew Jesus could save him and called out to Jesus to do so. *(St. Matthew 14:22-33)*

Salvation means to be saved from your sins and knowing that you are protected from the works and schemes of Satan and his demons. It also represents knowing, who you are in Christ and your position as it relates to the cares of this life. It keeps you from thinking carnally, and acting out in the flesh.

The carnal mind is a way of thinking that is actively hostile against God. Motivated by thoughts of worldly pleasures and pursuits; it energizes the flesh to pursue fulfillment of its animal appetites. Sin is the law or doctrine that governs this type of mind.

> Because the carnal mind is enmity against God: for it is not subject to the law of God, neither indeed can be.-Romans 8:7

Enmity" denotes a mutual and active hostility towards someone or something for a particular reason. The carnal mind and the construct of this world system are united in the same interests. The world has what the carnal state of a man desires and fulfills them. God and his law stand as the only opposition.

> Love not the world, neither the things that are in the world. If any man love the world, the love of the Father is not in him. For all that is in the world, the lust of the flesh, and the lust of the eyes, and the pride of life, is not of the Father, but is of the world. - 1 John 2:15-16

As followers of Jesus Christ we are mandated to abstain from fleshly lusts that wars against our souls *(1 Peter 2:11)*. Sin cannot be tolerated and must be dealt with accordingly. If a person is bound in sin openly or bears iniquity *(secret sins)*, Jesus provided the way of escape through the gospel of salvation. You must protect your head in battle. Keep the mind of Christ.

The Sword of the Spirit

> For the word of God is quick, and powerful, and sharper than any twoedged sword, piercing even to the dividing asunder of soul and spirit, and of the joints and marrow, and is a discerner of the thoughts and intents of the heart.-Hebrews 4:12

The Roman soldier's sword was designed to penetrate an opponent's shield and armor. It was sharply edged on both left and right sides. The sword of the Spirit is the Word of God.

You have to be skilled in the word of God and its usage. It is not enough to just know it. How many times have you seen in films, an armed hero enter a dark hall or cave, realizes that he needs light to light his way, and when he ignites it, all the monsters that are in that cave becomes aware of him and he aware of them and the a battle starts. During that battle, the light reveals a pathway for the hero to take. This is how the word of God works. It separates the light from the dark, exposing everything that is not like God.

> Thy word is a lamp unto my feet, and a light unto my path.-Psalms 119:105

The sword of the spirit of God will cut through all the defenses and counter the offenses that the enemy will use against your mind. Satan is the father of lies; the word of God is truth. Whatever Satan says to you, you counter against it with the word of truth. You must learn how to wield your sword or speak the word of God over your mind and situations. Speaking the word of God involves prayer, petitioning God according to His word.

Understand that in your life battles, there will be times when you will have to speak the word of God to your defense or offense. The result may cause more offenses against you, but you must remain vigilant and stand on the word of truth.

In following peace with all men, the word of God has the power to impart life and unity between those who work against you. When you speak the scripture, you must speak it in love. Your motivation behind your wielding must be right, for that, same word will one day judge you.

Through the word, Jesus brought deliverance to those who were bound and healing to those that were sick *(psalms 107:20)*. Those that challenged his ministry and beliefs, he responded by speaking the word of God. You must do the same.

Chapter Sixteen

Spiritual Weapons: Part 3 Prayer

And Jesus rebuked the devil; and he departed out of him: and the child was cured from that very hour. Then came the disciples to Jesus apart, and said, Why could not we cast him out. And Jesus said unto them, Because of your unbelief: for verily I say unto you, If ye have faith as a grain of mustard seed, ye shall say unto this mountain, Remove hence to yonder place; and it shall remove; and nothing shall be impossible unto you. Howbeit this kind goeth not out but by prayer and fasting. - St. Matthew 17:18-21

The disciples were trying to cast a devil out of a child but could not. Jesus told them that their unbelief was the cause of their failure. He gave them a cure for unbelief, both, which required personal sacrifice. Prayer is the offensive and defensive tool that holds all the armor of God together. Fasting makes prayer more effective.

In Apostle Paul's address to the Ephesian church, He exhorts them to "pray always." Prayer is the conduit of "communication with God." "Pray" defines how prayer is performed. "Supplication or Supplicate" defines the manner in which both pray and prayer is conducted.

Prayer

Prayer is more than simply communicating with God. It is a complex of spiritual ideas and levels of communication that are required for building your spirit man. Prayer to God is like a troop keeping communication with their captain. Without prayer, your armor for battle would be ineffective. In addition, the methods and tactics needed to defeat the enemy would go uncommunicated.

Prayer is Supplication.

A supplicating prayer is approaching God in a humble spirit, and making the request known. In Psalms 5:8, the psalmist prays for guidance in doing the right thing because of the persecution he was receiving from his enemies. He needed God's deliverance.

Supplicating prayer is asking for what you need from God. There is a saying among many Christians now that says, "Stop always asking God for things and start worshiping Him more." This teaching or saying is contrary to biblical doctrine, and will render you powerless before the enemy. Do not separate worship and prayer, both go hand in hand.

> And this is the confidence that we have in him, that, if we ask any thing according to his will, he heareth us: And if we know that he hear us, whatsoever we ask, we know that we have the petitions that we desired of him.-1 John 5:14-15

To petition God means that you want Him to change something in your life. It indicates a need and a trust that He has the resources that you need in order to overcome. He wants you to ask him.

> Ask, and it shall be given you; seek, and ye shall find; knock, and it shall be opened unto you: For every one that asketh receiveth; and he that seeketh findeth; and to him that knocketh it shall be opened. Or what man is there of you, whom if his son ask bread, will he give him a stone? Or if he ask a fish, will he give him a serpent? If ye then, being evil, know how to give good gifts unto your children, how much more shall your Father which is in heaven give good things to them that ask him?-St. Matthew 7:7-11

Note the contrast that Jesus makes between a sinful father and God, the Father. If sinful men provide for their children and desire to do so, how much more shall your Father, who is rich in mercy and full of grace, desire to bless you and answer your prayers? This leads us to the next aspect of prayer.

Prayer Is Having Faith

The idea of "asking God" in prayer is a strong indicator that you trust Him to accomplish your request and that He is capable of doing it. The prayer of faith is centered on the foundation of every promise that God has made to His children. It is one thing to know that God hears your prayers, but a greater assurance is added when you know He will answer.

> And whatsoever ye shall ask in my name, that will I do, that the Father may be glorified in the Son. If ye shall ask any thing in my name, I will do it.-St. John 14:13-14

Prayer is Worship

Praying with supplication, and faith, while knowing that God has promised to answer your prayers, removes fear, and doubt even in the heat of battle. Through these facets of prayer, you discover that God is more worthy of your respect, devotion, and love, because of His care for you. Knowing this brings Joy, thanksgiving and a desire to fellowship with God more and more. It draws you near to Him, lifting up holy hands in adoration, bowing down before His presence and submitting all that you are and have to Him in total submission.

> Give unto the LORD the glory due unto his name: bring an offering, and come before him: worship the LORD in the beauty of holiness.-1 Chronicles 16:29.

Prayer is Praise

Prayer is praising God for what He has done and what He is going to do. It is recognizing and acknowledging "out loud" that your God is mighty in battle and a strong deliverer. In praising God, thanksgiving is offered up to Him in advance, which is also an act of faith in the power of God before and in the midst of the battle.

Praise is also a mass annihilator of enemy forces. It is a weapon of mass destruction when you are surrounded by your enemies.

> And they rose early in the morning, and went forth into the wilderness of Tekoa: and as they went forth, Jehoshaphat stood and said, Hear me, O Judah, and ye inhabitants of Jerusalem;

Believe in the LORD your God, so shall ye be established; believe his prophets, so shall ye prosper. And when he had consulted with the people, he appointed singers unto the LORD, and that should praise the beauty of holiness, as they went out before the army, and to say, Praise the LORD; for his mercy endureth for ever. And when they began to sing and to praise, the LORD set ambushments against the children of Ammon, Moab, and mount Seir, which were come against Judah; and they were smitten. For the children of Ammon and Moab stood up against the inhabitants of mount Seir, utterly to slay and destroy them: and when they had made an end of the inhabitants of Seir, every one helped to destroy another. And when Judah came toward the watch tower in the wilderness, they looked unto the multitude, and, behold, they were dead bodies fallen to the earth, and none escaped. And when Jehoshaphat and his people came to take away the spoil of them, they found among them in abundance both riches with the dead bodies, and precious jewels, which they stripped off for themselves, more than they could carry away: and they were three days in gathering of the spoil, it was so much. And on the fourth day they assembled themselves in the valley of Berachah; for there they blessed the LORD: therefore the name of the same place was called, The valley of Berachah, unto this day. Then they returned, every man of Judah and Jerusalem, and Jehoshaphat in the forefront of them, to go again to Jerusalem with joy; for the LORD had made them to rejoice over their enemies. And they came to Jerusalem with psalteries and harps and trumpets unto the house of the LORD. And the fear of God was on all the kingdoms of those countries, when they had heard that the LORD fought against the enemies of Israel.-2 Chronicles 20:20-29

As you can see, prayer is not just "communicating with God" it is a system of methods that make-up the construct of communication in prayer. Now that you know what prayer is, you must know how to do it.

How to Pray

We have already discussed that praying is asking or petitioning God for what you need. However, there are various ways to pray that makes prayer even more dangerous to the enemy.

Unceasing Prayer

> Pray without ceasing. In everything give thanks: for this is the will of God in Christ Jesus concerning you.-1 Thessalonians 5:17-18

Unceasing prayer is the key to deliverance from satanic traps. In the books of Acts chapter 12:5-19, Herod rose up to persecute the church and killed James, John's brother. In order to gain more favor with the Jews, he imprisoned Peter. However, when Herod had resolved to kill Peter, the church prayed, "without ceasing." During the time of their prayer, God sent an angel and miraculously delivered Peter out of the prison bonds, escorted him pass the soldiers and through the Iron Gate, into the street. When Peter arrived at Marys' home, where they were gathered praying, Rhoda a young damsel, answered the door, saw that it was Peter, did not open the door, but ran to those who were praying, with her report. They assumed that Rhoda was crazy, but when they answered the door, they were shocked to see Peter. St. Luke 18:1 encourages us to pray always. Doing so will keep us encouraged, while we wait for His deliverance.

Develop a prayer life by whispering a prayer in your heart when in public and a place to pray alone when at home. You have to make the time to commune with God in prayer.

Intercessory Prayer

Intercessory prayer is seeking God on behalf of somebody else, even your enemies. When you are battling in warfare on your job, in your home or at church with individuals, intercessory prayer reminds you that your battle is against demon forces, not the people. Your weapon is not to retaliate with words or actions that are non-Christian. You are to battle evil in prayer to God.

Intercession indicates urgency. When you are persecuted, the judgment of God is on the head of the persecutor.

> Woe unto the world because of offences! for it must needs be that offences come; but woe to that man by whom the offence cometh!-St. Matthew 18:7

God has promised to revenge his elect, but you are not to expect your enemies to be destroyed. You are to pray and make them traitors to Satan's kingdom, by winning them over to holiness through intercession. Intercessory prayer is forgetting about yourself and praying that God would meet the need of others, even your enemies. In Exodus 8:28, Pharaoh, though he was an enemy of Moses, recognized the power of Moses's God and entreated him to intercede on his behalf. Intercessory prayer carries much weight of responsibility in your witness for Christ. God just does not want you to be delivered; He wants others, those who have suffered like you, even your enemies to experience the same. You must pray for others, even when you are seeking God for your own needs.

Binding and Loosing

> And I will give unto thee the keys of the kingdom of heaven: and whatsoever thou shalt bind on earth shall be bound in heaven: and whatsoever thou shalt loose on earth shall be loosed in heaven. Matthew 16:19.

Binding and loosing prayers demonstrate the power and authority of the Holy Ghost through what is called "declaring and/or decreeing." Jesus described this method as "keys to the kingdom."

The "Kingdom of God" is God's sovereign reign over the entire spiritual realm. This includes Satan's kingdom. Now God's sovereignty is not limited. It extends even over all the natural kingdoms of the world. Psalms 24:1 tells us *the earth is the Lord's and the fulness thereof, and they that dwell therein."* Everything is subject to God and is under His control.

"Power" in Acts 1:8 signifies jurisdiction and authority, again referring to Jesus definition of authority. "Keys" indicate access to releasing delegated authority, given by the Holy Ghost *(Acts 1:8)* to the Church of Jesus Christ, over the powers of the enemy.

Binding

Binding is handcuffing the enemy and stopping his current work and the influence that is working against you. Binding does not cast him out. Binding will give you temporary relief from the attack of the enemy, while you strategize your next move. If people are

164

working against you on your job, saying the words, "I bind the works of the enemy on my job in Jesus name" will stop his works and schemes temporarily. This is what it means, "to bind on earth."

Binding in heaven refers to your access to the kingdom of Satan." In this scripture, "Heaven" comes from the Greek term "ouranos" which means "sky" or "air." When you bind the devil with words on earth, you bind the prince of the power of "air," you bind him in the spiritual realm.

Loosing

Loosing refers to breaking the bondages of the enemy and going free from the demons influence. Whether it is against you or in the life of someone, you are interceding for. Remember the words Jesus spoke to the woman with the issue of blood? He said, "Woman, thou art "loosed" from thine infirmity." Immediately, she was made straight.

Application

If the enemy is attacking your life and attempting to strip you of all of what God has given you, you must bind him and stop his work. Afterwards, you have to speak the words that loose the demonic from your situation and then seek God on how to restore. If you are constantly being drawn into sexual sin, constantly running to your computer, partner in adultery for sexual gratification, or maybe an unbridled desire for cigarettes, drinking, etc..., If you are in a spirit-filled church, I recommend you speak to your leader about the problem. Collaborate with him for your deliverance; have him pray over you to loose the powers of the enemy from over your life. You need something greater than you to break the bondage.

When witnessing you can bind the evil spirit that will cause a person to turn a deaf ear to your words, giving you access to reach him with the gospel. If they confess, you can then bind the spirits and cast them out, winning the soul completely over to Christ. In any area of your life that is hindered by the powers of darkness, God has given you authority to stop it and cast it out.

Turn to God in prayer and reap the benefits of spiritual authority.

Acquaint now thyself with him, and be at peace: thereby good shall come unto thee. Receive, I pray thee, the law from his mouth, and lay up his words in thine heart. If thou return to the Almighty, thou shalt be built up, thou shalt put away iniquity far from thy tabernacles. Then shalt thou lay up gold as dust and the gold of Ophir as the stones of the brooks. Yea, the Almighty shall be thy defence, and thou shalt have plenty of silver. For then shalt thou have thy delight in the Almighty, and shalt lift up thy face unto God. Thou shalt make thy prayer unto him, and he shall hear thee, and thou shalt pay thy vows. Thou shalt also decree a thing, and it shall be established unto thee: and the light shall shine upon thy ways. When men are cast down, then thou shalt say, There is lifting up; and he shall save the humble person. He shall deliver the island of the innocent: and it is delivered by the pureness of thine hands.-Job 22:20-30.

Chapter Seventeen

Spiritual Weapons: Part 3 Fasting

When you pray, you have to incorporate fasting. Jesus told his disciples in St. Matthew 17:21 that mountain moving power comes with prayer and fasting. Both practices, together cures unbelief.

In St. Matthew Chapter 4:2, after Jesus was baptized in the Holy Ghost, he fasted for forty days and nights. The purpose of the fast was to prepare him for ministry. It is not just a mere religious practice; it is an intense method of seeking God. It has significant reasons for its performance.

> But as for me, when they were sick, my clothing was sackcloth: I humbled my soul with fasting; and my prayer returned into mine own bosom.-Psalms 35:13

Fasting humbles the soul before God. Some people approach God in a religious boast of pride, as if God owes them because of their righteous performance. Fasting is like an urgent call for help from God in times of distress, sickness, grief, and repentance. It designates a total dependence on God and His power. It is for spiritual breakthrough.

Fasting Under Heavy Attack

When under heavy spiritual attack, fasting is necessary and causes God to move against Satan's plans that are executed against you. In the book of Esther, when Haman set out to destroy the Jews, they fasted *(4:2-3)* and in an answer to their cry, God rose up Esther to go before the king, to inform him of the matter. Before Esther approached the king, she proclaimed a fast for three days *(vs 16-17)*. Because of their fasting and prayers, God turned the plan of Haman in favor of Esther and the Jews. The very gallows that Haman built to have the Jews hung on, he was hung there for all to see.

Fasting For Direction

In Exodus 34:27-28, Moses fasted forty days and forty nights, before the Lord and received commandments concerning the tabernacle and its ordinances for worship and sacrifice.

Loosing the Bands of Wickedness

> Is not this the fast that I have chosen? to loose the bands of wickedness, to undo the heavy burdens, and to let the oppressed go free, and that ye break every yoke? Is it not to deal thy bread to the hungry, and that thou bring the poor that are cast out to thy house? when thou seest the naked, that thou cover him; and that thou hide not thyself from thine own flesh?- Isaiah 58:6-7

Here we find nine reasons for fasting. All of which deals with breaking the yokes of oppression. The bands represent the different types of yokes inflicted on you through the wickedness of men who are energized by evil spirits. In the book of Nehemiah, chapter five, the people of God were oppressed through greed by the Jews. The country was in an economic slump and suffering a famine, the people mortgaged off their lands, homes, and their vineyards *(businesses),* in order to buy corn for feeding their families. Some had taken out loans against their properties, even went to work for the Jews, but still there was not enough pay. Some of their children were being sold into slavery in order to support themselves during the famine, but could not pay the tribute charged to release them.

These actions placed heavy burdens on the people, due to the yoke of unlawful debts. This caused the people to be oppressed. Fasting with prayer will break the yoke of wickedness inflicted against you.

Do you find yourself in positions where you are:

- Constantly being fired from Jobs
- Finances are always diminishing.

- Constantly suffering cycles of sickness and disease
- Can't seem to break free from entangling situations
- Suffering constant family issues

These are things designed to burden and oppress. The fast that God calls for breaks these cycles. In Isaiah 58:7, we find that the God chosen fasts brings provision by breaking the cycle of poverty, enabling you to not only be blessed, but also make you a conduit of blessings to those who are less fortunate.

> Is it not to deal thy bread to the hungry, and that thou bring the poor that are cast out to thy house? when thou seest the naked, that thou cover him; and that thou hide not thyself from thine own flesh?-Isaiah 58:7

The God chosen fast will break the cycles of sickness and lead you into a healthy lifestyle. It will also enhance your spiritual life and power, enabling you to go forth in your purpose and destiny. God's presence will manifest in your life, enabling you to live a life of joy under His protection.

> Then shall thy light break forth as the morning, and thine health shall spring forth speedily: and thy righteousness shall go before thee; the glory of the LORD shall be thy reward.-Isaiah 58:8

This fast will give you an assurance of answered prayer in midst of troubles and slander. When the evil day of tribulation comes into your life, your righteousness will shine through the darkness, lighting your pathway to victory. God will guide you and instruct you, using you as a tool of deliverance in the lives of others.

> Then shalt thou call, and the LORD shall answer; thou shalt cry, and he shall say, Here I am. If thou take away from the midst of thee the yoke, the putting forth of the finger, and speaking vanity; And if thou draw out thy soul to the hungry, and satisfy the afflicted soul; then shall thy light rise in obscurity, and thy darkness be as the noon day: And the LORD shall guide thee continually, and satisfy thy soul in drought, and make fat thy bones: and thou shalt be like a watered garden, and like a spring of water, whose waters fail not. And they that shall be of thee shall build the old waste places: thou shalt raise up the

foundations of many generations; and thou shalt be called, The repairer of the breach, The restorer of paths to dwell in.-Isaiah 58:9-12

Fasting Crucifies the Flesh

Fasting with prayer crucifies or kills fleshly desires by bringing them under subjection to Gods word; nullifying the influence of sin that would work against you.

> Knowing this, that our old man is crucified with him, that the body of sin might be destroyed, that henceforth we should not serve sin. For he that is dead is freed from sin. Romans 6:6-7

The old man is the old you. It is the old desires that move you to yield to the temptations of sin, which you once enjoyed. Fasting, praying, and studying the word of God subjects you to obey and creates a sensitivity to the voice and guidance of the Spirit of God. Fasting must be done through the Spirit of God.

> For if ye live after the flesh, ye shall die: but if ye through the Spirit do mortify the deeds of the body, ye shall live.-Romans 8:13

Sin will always strive to bring you back under its bondage. Fasting under the power of the Holy Ghost enhances your ability to live righteously, overcoming sin's influence.

How to Fast

> Moreover, when ye fast, be not, as the hypocrites, of a sad countenance: for they disfigure their faces, that they may appear unto men to fast. Verily I say unto you, They have their reward. But thou, when thou fastest, anoint thine head, and wash thy face; That thou appear not unto men to fast, but unto thy Father which is in secret: and thy Father, which seeth in secret, shall reward thee openly.-St. Matthew 6:16-18

Fasting is exercising a spiritual assault on the forces of darkness. Therefore, the process of performing a fast must be done properly, if you expect results. Now here are three types of fasts:

- **The Absolute Fast** or the **Jesus Fast**: No Food and water (This fast is for power)
- **The Daniel Fast**: involves eating only vegetables. This fast is for health reasons.
- There is a fast where you <u>abstain from food only</u>, and yet drink water.

As stated when you begin your fast, like prayer you must do it in secret, by washing your face and anointing your head with oil. You must not appear as if you are struggling with your fast in public. Next, choose a period for fasting. Make sure during that time, you read your word and get in a prayer, even if it is in your mind. As for the length, there is no set time. You must choose a timeframe that would be a considerable time for sacrifice to God. You must fast in faith. The sincerity counts. Also, remember that the bigger the sacrifice, the greater the blessing. You are not fasting to become more spiritual you are fasting because you are spiritual.

Exhortations

I exhort you to remember these points as you take your journey in deliverance and on to spiritual prosperity in God.

Don't Play the Victim

Be honest with yourself. No matter the situation you are in, you are responsible for your own actions. Eve was the first in transgressing the word of God, but the commandment was given to Adam. When God inquired about their iniquity, Adam played the victim by blaming Eve. God still punished Adam for his actions and he will hold you accountable for yours.

Do not seek the sympathy from others because of your own mistakes. Exercise spiritual responsibility by doing what you know is right. Hone up to your mistakes and sins. Do not cover them. Confess them. If you fall, get up, and keep moving forward.

Forgive Yourself

> Therefore if any man be in Christ, he is a new creature: old things are passed away; behold, all things are become new. And all things are of God, who hath reconciled us to himself by Jesus Christ, and hath given to us the ministry of reconciliation;-2 Corinthians 5:17-18

You are a new creation. Your past is no more. Since God has forgiven you, there is no reason to torment yourself, by persistently conjuring up your past. When you fail to forgive yourself, you deny the work of the cross. You allow yourself to live in guilt of things that God has forgiven.

Your sin debt has been paid in full. Rejoice, rejoice, again I say rejoice. You have a new life, a fresh start.

Avoid Distractions

> I will meditate in thy precepts, and have respect unto thy ways.- Psalms 119:15

Stay focused in your journey and spiritual growth. Old habits and friends will always cross your path, seeking to dissuade you from what God has for you. Keep your mind on the word of God. Read it, study it, and practice it. Stay prayerful.

Find a Good Church

> Not forsaking the assembling of ourselves together, as the manner of some is; but exhorting one another: and so much the more, as ye see the day approaching. - Hebrews 10:25

I cannot express enough how important it is for you to find a good spirit filled church that teaches the Holiness of God according to the word of God. Your faith increases by hearing the word:

> How then shall they call on him in whom they have not believed? and how shall they believe in him of whom they have not heard? and how shall they hear without a preacher? And how shall they preach, except they be sent? as it is written, How beautiful are the feet of them that preach the gospel of peace, and bring glad tidings of good things! But they have not all obeyed the gospel. For Esaias saith, Lord, who hath believed our report. So then faith cometh by hearing, and hearing by the word of God.- Romans 10:14-20

A healthy church is guided by a preacher who does not compromise the gospel but and is bold in the face of the enemy. This is the only kind of preacher that can build your faith. Go to church.

I pray that this book has been blessing to you. God Bless.

About The Author

Monte L. Monk is a passionate gospel teacher and evangelist. He accepted Jesus Christ as his personal Lord and Savior at the age of eighteen. Two years later, he was called to the gospel ministry. He now resides in Dallas TX with his wife, Teresa and his daughter, Tamesha Monk.

He is an avid reader and researcher of the scriptures. He believes that the answers to mankind's problems are found in the word of God. He is passionate about winning souls for Christ and promoting the kingdom of God.

www.ingramcontent.com/pod-product-compliance
Lightning Source LLC
LaVergne TN
LVHW041251080426
835510LV00009B/685